Ralph Fiennes

I have been lucky enougl
– and have felt hugely en;   _. ʍɾɵᴄise
insight into the infinite cha.   ᵧᵤᵤ ᴜᵣ communicating a text
on stage.

This book is an invaluable guide to her work, offering clearly explained exercises that can provoke further discovery of any role or spoken text. It is a great resource for actors and directors.

Simon Godwin

Jeannette Nelson's revelatory relationship to language is, quite simply, life-changing. No one has helped me understand Shakespeare better than Jeannette. Her meticulous, empowering approach is irresistible and inspiring.

Wiping away centuries of confusion, Jeannette brings Shakespeare alive once more. More than anyone working in theatre today, she brings us close to the intricate workings of Shakespeare's thoughts. In this immensely practical and grounded book, we can all become better actors, better speakers, better thinkers.

Jeannette has fostered a generation of great Shakespearean actors – all united by clarity, honesty and humanity. This book demonstrates how to become one of them.

When I met Jeannette, I was searching for a way of bringing classical language to life. I was lost in theories and academia. Her approach was a revelation – her gentle power, her deep insight, her practical way of making words and ideas necessary were career-changing. Collaborating on *Twelfth Night, Antony and Cleopatra* and the film of *Romeo and Juliet* was transformative. This radiant and vital book means everyone can now access her uplifting approach to unlocking the power and glory of language.

Sophie Okonedo

I spent many months working with Jeannette on *Antony and Cleopatra*. She taught me so much. By the time I came to perform I felt like I had enormous flexibility in my voice and could persuade anybody to do anything!

Jeannette Nelson

Keeping
It Active

A Practical Guide to
Rhetoric in Performance

Foreword by Josie Rourke

NICK HERN BOOKS
London
www.nickhernbooks.co.uk

A Nick Hern Book

Keeping It Active
first published in Great Britain in 2022
by Nick Hern Books Limited,
The Glasshouse, 49a Goldhawk Road, London W12 8QP

Copyright © 2022 Jeannette Nelson
Foreword copyright © 2022 Josie Rourke

Jeannette Nelson has asserted her moral right
to be identified as the author of this work

Designed and typeset by Nick Hern Books, London
Printed and bound in Great Britain by
Severn, Gloucester

A CIP catalogue record for this book is available
from the British Library

ISBN 978 1 84842 936 9

Contents

Foreword by Josie Rourke...vii

Introduction...xi
Preparing the Play: Where Do We Start?..............................xviii
Exercises with Texts...xx

1   Rhetoric...1
    A Little History..3
    Rhetorical Strategies...5
    Political Rhetoric...8

2   Rhetoric in Drama...15
    The Use of Rhetorical Strategies in Dramatic Speeches..17
    Playing the Strategies..24
    Rhetorical Strategies in Dialogue....................................25

3   Other Rhetorical Strategies in Drama...........................35
    Appropriating Your Opponent's Vocabulary.....................37
    Revealing the Themes of the Play....................................47
    Dislocation...58
    Open and Closed Questions...59
    Status in Dialogue..65
    Listening...68

4   Rhetorical Patterns..73
    Three-part Structure: Storytelling.....................................75
    Tricolon or The Rule of Three...86
    Oppositions..89

5   Word Play, Imagery and Figurative Language............101
    Metaphor and Simile...103
    Expressing Feelings Actively...106
    Alliteration and Assonance...110

6 Code Language..**117**

**7 Showing Several Rhetorical Devices
    Being Used Within the Scene**.......................................**131**

8 The Use of Punctuation in Rhetoric............................**155**
    Colon...157
    Semi-colon...158
    A Word of Warning About Commas...............................159

Conclusion...**163**

Acknowledgements..**168**

About the Author..**169**

Foreword
Josie Rourke

I was recently a part of a panel discussing ethics in modern politics. The audience was mainly establishment figures: politicians and civil servants. During the Q&A, someone raised their hand and asked how, as a politician, one could be 'authentic'.

It's a tricky one because you can – of course – be authentically awful. I think the questioner was asking how politicians make themselves trusted and believed. As Jeannette points out, in this great book: hundreds of years ago, the answer to that would have been 'with rhetoric'.

It's a cliché for me to write that rhetoric is a dirty word. Like many dirty words, rhetoric is a powerful and powerfully misused term. Often, the accusation 'That's just rhetoric' is levelled at the idea itself rather than the techniques of argument that 'rhetoric' describes. When we say 'rhetoric' but mean 'lying', we're finding fault with the car when we meant to criticise the route its driver has chosen.

But can we blame us? As a director who has worked a lot on plays containing rhetoric, I'm not sure that the 'Rhetoric doesn't hurt people; people hurt people' notion always holds. To understand how to make the shape of an argument can make you more argumentative. Once you know how it works and can manipulate the blocks you're playing with, it's addictive. It can make you into a full-time salesperson.

For me, it's a pressing question. If the twentieth century decided everything was for sale, that having gone well, the twenty-first century turned its attention to selling the self.

There's no better moment to interrogate how that's done and – by extension – what doing it does to the self.

As this excellent book outlines, rhetoric is everywhere. It's not simply in the parliament, the press conference and the court; it's in the workplace, the home and the family. There's no argument, classical or modern, in a play that isn't informed and helped by Jeannette's work.

Thinking back to the beginning of that work, with Jeannette and my friend Benet Brandreth, whom she mentions in this book: this idea of 'rhetoric' was a big, lovely learning curve for me. Both Jeannette and Benet were teaching me and the acting company concepts we'd not studied before.

It's important that I can lay this out here because I also think that we're in a cultural and political moment of acute awareness as to how certain types of education are aligned with certain conditions of privilege. Put simply, there are not debating societies in all schools.

What I'd say of this great work on rhetoric is that there's some stuff that we may not be taught at school but that doesn't mean it's not our cultural inheritance. One of the things I find to be so moving about this book is Jeannette Nelson's steady and generous determination that we should share and know everything about acting.

Equally, one of the things I admire so much about British actors is their appetite for knowledge and continuing training. This system of thinking about text is fascinating; useful; political and should be accessible to all. I'm so grateful to Jeannette for her laying it out in this book with such great clarity and her compassionate understanding of the whole craft of acting.

Josie Rourke was born in Salford. She is the former Artistic Director of the Bush Theatre and the Donmar Warehouse. She served as a Non-Executive Director of Channel 4. Her current roles include Vice President of the London Library.

Josie Rourke was born in Salford. She is Artistic Director of the Bush Theatre and the Donmar Warehouse. She served as a Non-Executive Director of Chapter, and most recently as a President of the London Library

Introduction

RHETORIC IS ABOUT MAKING
SURE YOU ARE HEARD,
UNDERSTOOD AND BELIEVED.

Standing in the bar of a London theatre one evening, at the interval of a new play, I overheard a conversation between three people that went something like this:

A: I'm struggling with this, the rhetoric is so overdone. I'm not sure I'll go back in for the second half.

B: Well, you have to get your ear in, don't you? But I think it's worth it. I'd say it's not overdone, I'd say it's rich.

C: I think the problem is that everyone is speaking a different rhetoric so no one is talking to anyone.

Whatever the problem with this particular play, I think the real problem was that each speaker meant something different when they spoke about rhetoric, and only speaker C got anywhere near the real meaning. Rhetoric isn't a general catch-all term for spoken language: it's about how we communicate; how we make an impact on our listeners; and specifically, what language we choose to try to make things happen. If you are an actor, or a director, or a teacher of acting or theatre studies, then you need to know about rhetoric, because it is the Art of Persuasion. In this book I'm going to tell you something about it, how it works in plays, and how it can transform the work of actors.

I think that every time you open your mouth on stage (and maybe in life) you are trying to persuade somebody of something: an idea or point of view, in order to be better understood or to change someone's mind; to get what you want; or to make something happen. Characters in plays often, consciously or unconsciously, employ various rhetorical techniques to try to gain or maintain ground in some way. Whether that be socially, politically, ethically or emotionally, it is interesting and empowering to discover who can and who cannot, who does and who does not play the rhetorical word game.

In 2005, I was voice coach for the Royal Shakespeare Company's 'Gunpowder' season in the Swan Theatre in Stratford-upon-Avon. As part of that season, Josie Rourke directed a production of *Believe What You Will* (original title *Believe As You List*) by Philip Massinger which changed my way of thinking about and working with texts forever. During rehearsals she invited the barrister Benet Brandreth to come and talk to the company about rhetoric. That day he shone a new light on everything I had ever learned about voice and text for theatre. That illumination has steered my work ever since, and I want to share it with you here.

Applying voice work to the text – to the words and thoughts of individual characters – has always been an essential element of a theatre voice coach's job. Up to that point I had been quite successful, I think, but, now that I have more understanding of the true purpose of rhetoric, I have been able to refine my approach to working with the language of plays, and create a simplicity and unity to the work that is easily understood and used by actors. The results are productions that have been praised for their clarity. When an actor understands and actively uses a play's rhetoric, it works for them, their character and the audience.

You may think that rhetoric is something old-fashioned and therefore only relevant to older works, like classical Greek plays or those of Shakespeare and his contemporaries. It is not. My aim in this book is to help you to see that rhetoric – language used persuasively and strategically – is to be found in the dialogue and speeches of plays from all periods and in all forms. I hear rhetoric alive and very active in every play I read, listen to or work with, and I am going to share that perspective with you. You will see that, if an actor can recognise and understand the rhetoric, they can allow the character they are playing to own it, and by doing so, they can get deeper into the mind and under the skin of that character. You will also find that working with the rhetoric will greatly aid the clarity and audibility of the dialogue, as it is a way of actively using the text to communicate with other characters in the play, as well as with the audience.

Although I have been a theatre voice coach for over thirty years, my journey to that day in the rehearsal room in Stratford had begun in 1997 when I was the first voice coach at Shakespeare's Globe Theatre, located in Southwark, on the south bank of the River Thames in London. The Globe is a re-creation of a theatre that Shakespeare had played in and part owned. If you have seen plays there, you will know how beautiful it is and that it enjoys its authenticity as a building. However, for a modern actor, using modern acting techniques, it is not an easy place in which to make yourself heard clearly by every member of the audience. Even in the original building it can't have been easy: these playhouses were very difficult spaces in which to focus on the play. They were crowded with an audience that wasn't simply seated in an orderly fashion: there were people walking around; there were people selling fruit and other snacks; the 'groundlings' were standing or perhaps milling around in front of the stage; the place was open to the elements and the wooden structure was noisy to walk on. Much of that is true of the modern version too. The audience in the original theatre was very socially varied, and the majority were not literate. However, they would say they were going to *hear* a play, not *see* a play, as we say today.

In the modern Globe Theatre, audiences are rather better behaved, but the actors still have to contend with some noise and distractions from inside the building, as well as the intrusive sounds of a modern capital city coming from outside, including aircraft, motorbikes and, when I was there, bridge-building! So, I spent a great deal of time thinking about how I could best focus my work to help the actors perform successfully in that acoustically challenging space. Eventually, my thoughts turned to a very basic question: why had the playwrights writing for those theatres used verse drama? Knowing that verse drama was the dominant form of early European plays and that most of the time they had been performed outside, I realised the simple fact that verse was and still is a very powerful form with which to reach out to an audience. Verse, with all its stylistic elements, can really help the audience to hear the play; to follow the complexities of plot and to engage with the feelings and motivations of characters. Especially in the open air and in those noisy, busy Elizabethan theatres.

Despite this realisation, I wonder what you'll think when I tell you I never go to a Shakespeare production to hear poetry. I go to hear ideas and stories. I want to tell you I'm not interested in how well an actor speaks the verse; I'm interested in plays that move me in some way because of how characters think and speak in the situations in which they find themselves. I'm interested in hearing the depth and complexity of the human mind that Shakespeare presents to us as his characters try to make their way through the equally complex world they find themselves in. A world that is as complex today.

This doesn't mean that I don't look at, use, or care about the style, form and content of poetic texts. For me, everything that is considered to be poetry in Shakespeare, and in other writers who use a poetic form of drama, is rhetoric: language designed to persuade. Alliteration, assonance, rhyme, repetition, metre, antithesis, imagery, the form and shape of the poetry are all hooks to draw the listener's ear to the meaning of the text. My work engages with all the rhetorical/poetical elements of the text but not for the sake of poetry or beauty, but to empower the actor and their character to own the language and the ideas it carries and use it to be heard. When an actor does this, they play the text very actively, focusing what they are saying on the person or people they are talking to in order to be heard and understood by them. This then goes a long way towards the audience really *hearing* the play, and quite possibly being moved or changed by what they hear.

Being 'active' with a character's thoughts, speaking 'actively', and 'actioning' your lines have become almost standard practice for British actors and directors today. The ideas are firmly based in Stanislavsky's techniques and have been made popular through the work of the director Max Stafford-Clark, with whom I have had the pleasure of working many times. Max outlined his 'actioning' method in his book *Letters to George* (Nick Hern Books, 1989). He introduced the idea of using a transitive verb to describe how characters, moment by moment, try to affect, or change the mind of, the people they are speaking to. I want to show you in this book that, when an actor thinks about being persuasive when their character speaks, they will also be using their words actively. Working with rhetoric is absolutely in line with this modern British acting practice, and plays very well alongside it.

I am indebted to Josie Rourke more that she will ever know, and also to the many talented actors who have taken this understanding of rhetoric into their wonderful performances.

I am also deeply grateful to the directors who have since allowed me and encouraged me to work in this way. In particular Dominic Cooke, Marianne Elliott, Simon Godwin, Nicholas Hytner, Rufus Norris and Ian Rickson.

Preparing the Play: Where Do We Start?

Where do you start when you have been cast in a play, or if you are preparing to direct a play? When you've read the text and got a sense of the story, how do you explore the characters? How do you find your way into a part? If you are an actor, you probably look through the play to see what other characters say about your character, and what your character says about themselves. You might begin to think through a backstory to fill the character's life experience and what brought them to the point where they enter the play. As you begin to rehearse you will start to explore how they feel; what is their emotional truth. You may also be thinking about subtext and what is not being said.

When I look at a piece of playtext or listen to it spoken, I look for or listen for structure and patterns in the language. This is the way I discover the characters and the drama. I look for the way people explain themselves, through imagery and ideas. I see and hear where words are repeated or shared between characters; where they question and answer; where they listen or don't listen; and whether they hear what's being said to them or not. I discover how characters use vocabulary and idiom, and whether it unites people or divides them. I look for where their linguistic ammunition lies, and if and when they use it. I explore how characters lay out their thoughts, ideas and needs to each other, and I look for how they try to make things happen; how they try to persuade others to do, feel or think certain things. I follow the characters' language journeys through the drama, and I am looking for how they use rhetoric. I would like to introduce you to this and to the way I help actors find and use some of the rhetorical strategies to be found in plays. I will be sharing my way of thinking, my way of unlocking the language of a text, and how the actors and I can explore and play with what we find.

In my opinion, there is danger in an actor dwelling too much upon what individual words mean to them. It is a style of speaking that is often encouraged when working with Shakespeare. This is the idea that, in order to move the audience, the actor must realise the full emotional potential of the words Shakespeare has written. This can result in the actor being more concerned about how they or their character feels than they are about the effect their words are having on the person or people they are speaking to. Speech then tends to become reflective and passive, and the whole event can be very dull and often hard to follow. It can leave the audience cold or even irritated, as they witness the actor wrenching the language from their bodies.

In my experience, if an actor/character chooses to talk to themself on stage, the audience will never hear clearly what they are saying. Of course, I understand that there will be many moments when an actor instinctively wants to speak the words, or even a single word, reflectively or perhaps with a sense of the personal enjoyment of their character. However, I know that when this happens, the words are rarely heard clearly by the audience, especially in large theatres. Even in a soliloquy I feel it is important that the actor addresses someone or something (the audience, God, the universe). Then there is someone with whom to work out their thoughts: a focus for their argument. In doing so the language becomes active and moves the character and the play forward, and takes the audience with them.

In addition, when the rhetorical elements are understood by an actor and played dynamically, they can also reveal character and support the play's subtext and supra-text in a powerful way.

Exercises with Texts

In this book I am going to introduce you to some of the rhetorical strategies dramatists have given and are still giving their characters: strategies with which they move forward through the drama of the life they are sharing with us. Then I am going to show you some of the exercises I give to the actors I work with, to help them explore these strategies and use them to the full. I will also show you how other, perhaps more familiar, linguistic elements can be used persuasively, and I will give you further exercises to explore and define these elements.

These exercises are quite simple and usually in some way physical. When actors use their bodies in conjunction with the spoken word, it helps them to see and feel the structure of arguments very clearly. They are not strenuous exercises – I use them with actors of all ages and all physical conditions. As you will see, the exercises generally follow a similar pattern: they are designed to unlock the journey and the geography of thoughts and strategies found in the language of the play – and to unlock how characters debate, persuade, provoke and transform in some way, each other, themselves or their fate.

The work of the great Cicely Berry is the inspiration for many of these exercises. I was lucky enough to be employed by the Royal Shakespeare Company when she was still very active there. Her work was first introduced to me by David Carey when I trained as a voice coach at Central School of Speech and Drama.

1.

Rhetoric

RHETORIC IS THE ART OF
PERSUASION, DESIGNED FOR
DEBATE AND THE EXCHANGE
OF IDEAS.

Today the word 'rhetoric' seems to carry negative connotations; to imply manipulation, deceit or just petty wordplay; the tool of the political spin doctor, producing sound bites for media consumption. It is rarely associated with truth.

But rhetoric is the Art of Persuasion, designed for debate and the exchange of ideas. It is a way of understanding and using powerful language: language that will get into the ear and the imagination of the listener. Once you know a bit about it, you will realise that we use rhetoric all the time. In this book I will reveal some rhetorical techniques, and I will show you them used first in political speeches and then in plays. I believe you will understand them very easily. You may even find some of them are familiar to you but perhaps you had not heard them described as rhetoric. I also believe you will probably hear some of them spoken to you or even coming from your own mouth.

A Little History

Speaking appropriately and skilfully has been valued throughout history. In pre-literate oral societies, history and culture were celebrated and passed on through storytelling. Within many of these stories, heroic leaders were admired for the way they could motivate and excite their soldiers and followers through inspirational speech. In the few texts that survive we find out that the ancient Egyptians admired eloquence. The *Instruction Addressed to King Merikare* states:

> If you are skilled in speech, you will win,
> The tongue is a (king's) sword;

Speaking is stronger than all fighting,
The skilful is not overcome.

In another ancient Egyptian text, *The Tale of the Shipwrecked Sailor*, the servant says to his master, 'A man's mouth can save him. His speech makes one forgive him.' The Chinese philosopher Confucius also spoke of the power of language. In *The Analects* he states that 'The sole function of speech is to communicate ideas clearly,' and that, 'Without knowing the force of words, it is impossible to know more.' Isn't that wonderful? Statements from Confucius could be mottos for me, a modern voice coach.

Rhetoric as we know it today was first developed for the arguing of cases brought to law. Its seeds were sown in Ancient Greece by a group of itinerant teachers called the Sophists (the best known of whom are Gorgias and Isocrates), who travelled through the country, teaching oratorical skills. Its early flowering was in the Assembly and the law courts of Athens. There, as the idea of government by the people evolved, the ability to speak so as to be heard and to persuade became vital and often a matter of life and death.

Aristotle was the student of the great philosopher Plato and, although there are earlier texts mentioning persuasive language, he was the first to write about rhetoric as a structured discipline. His propositions were themselves debated and contested by the teachers and philosophers who followed him: primarily Demosthenes in Greece, and Cicero and Quintilian in Rome. Those that showed skill in persuasive speaking began to teach others, but it was Aristotle who wrote the manual. His treatise *The Art of Rhetoric* sets out structures, styles and strategies that became the blueprint for all further study of the discipline. It continues to be so today.

Shakespeare and his contemporaries studied rhetoric in school, which is evident throughout their plays. On one level you can see that Shakespeare's sonnets are exercises in rhetoric, each of them containing little debates on a particular subject. Some of them fall into groups, where he has taken an idea or conceit and worked it persuasively in several different ways. Many of them are clearly addressed to a particular person.

Whatever the current distrust of rhetoric, we hear it all around us. From the TV to the Old Bailey, from the pub to the Houses of Parliament, from the Lincoln Memorial to Hyde Park Corner, you can hear rhetoric in practice: the clever, acute TV advertising campaign, the well-told shaggy dog story, the barrister's summing up and the politician's motion. And you can also hear it on the stage in plays old and new. It is certainly not only in the classical canon of plays that we see the use of rhetoric today; in fact, I see it in some form in every play I work with. Some writers are perhaps more consciously aware of it than others, but if an actor learns to recognise the techniques, it can help them first of all to get into the mind of their character and, most important from my point of view, it helps them to own their character's language, and to use it powerfully to convey thoughts and arguments. It answers the question 'What am I really talking about?'

Rhetorical Strategies: Ethos, Pathos and Logos

Aristotle stated that there are three main strategies a speaker could use to argue his point: **Ethos**, **Pathos** or **Logos**. Sorry to spring a little Greek upon you all of a sudden, here is an explanation of these terms:

Ethos is the speaker presenting themself as having an authentic personal character which supports the credibility of their argument. This can happen in many ways. The speaker could remind their listeners of their personal life experience, their reputation, their family history or of some specific connection they have with their subject. In other words, they are presenting their credentials.

So, if you are the speaker, this is about you; why you can be trusted and believed.

Pathos is used to stir the emotions of the listeners, to make them feel something about the argument or situation. It could be excitement, joy or empathy. It could be indignation, remorse or horror. But it is always about affecting the *listeners'* feelings, not primarily about the speaker's own.

We don't have to look very far to see how powerful it can be to use an argument that touches the feelings of an audience. Political rhetoric shows us how the crowd can be roused to a passionate response on hearing highly emotive language. Even in television talent shows, the audience will cheer and applaud when the singer reaches the high, emotional point of their song.

Logos is used to back up an argument with evidence: laying out facts (whether or not they are true) to prove or support a point. It appeals to reason or intellect and shows why you are right or speaking the truth.

In simple terms I see these three ways of arguing as through:

Authenticity – Emotion – Facts

I'll explain these a little further, and I'm going to continue to use the Greek as these terms are simple and direct.

If a speaker at a local Planning Meeting wishes to prevent the development of a supermarket, he might begin using **Ethos** to say, '*You know me. My family have lived in this town for generations, and my mother's father was your minister.*' He might then lay out the facts as he wishes them to be seen using **Logos**. He could say, '*We already have three supermarkets in this town, and the volume of traffic over the bridge has increased incrementally. Now it takes school buses half an hour to get to the town centre when it used to take fifteen minutes.*' He might continue with **Pathos**: '*Do you want your historic town centre to have its heart cut out by big developers who don't live here and have no idea what the local community of shops and shopowners means to us?*'

In my imaginary Planning Meeting, the first speaker draws upon one of these elements at a time to affect his listeners and to persuade them that his is the right side to take.

Someone opposing him might put forward his own arguments in reply, but a more powerful, rhetorical first response would be to pick up the points his opponent has made and then turn them to his own advantage. For example: '*The former speaker's family may have their roots in this town, but they are looking to the past. I'm a modern man, living in the real world and I want to bring us into the twenty-first century*' (**Ethos**). '*My supermarket will bring in customers from a twenty-mile radius who will also bring trade to your shops. In addition we will be creating three hundred new jobs for the people of this town*' (**Logos**). '*We won't be cutting the heart out of your historic town; we'll be bringing new blood and new life to invigorate your marketplace and your community*' (**Pathos**) – where he takes his opponent's metaphor and makes it his own: '*Do you want your historic town centre to

7

have its heart cut out?' countered with *'We won't be cutting the heart out... we'll be bringing new blood and new life...'*

He might then go on and introduce new arguments which, if his opponent is clever enough, he will then himself turn back to his advantage.

Political Rhetoric

In political speech writing, these elements are often very clear. The speaker needs to present himself as someone his listeners can trust, and he needs to persuade them that he has a strong connection with the issues he's arguing for. He also needs to present the listeners with evidence to back up his argument, showing that he knows what he is talking about and can argue with the facts. However, working on the feelings, the emotions of listeners is always very powerful and will often have more impact than either of the other two methods. Today we all know the power of 'fake news'!

In recent years, one of the most prominent political rhetoricians has been, of course, President Barack Obama. It is worth looking at his speeches to see how distinctively and powerfully he uses the three strategies. I've chosen an early section from one of them: his acceptance speech at the Democratic Convention in Denver, Colorado, on 28 August 2008. After he has thanked the chairman and his fellow nominees, he begins, as did the Greeks, with **Ethos**: his personal history, linked to the history of the people of America.

> Four years ago, I stood before you and told you my story – of the brief union between a young man from Kenya and a young woman from Kansas who weren't well-off or well-known, but shared a belief that in

America, their son could achieve whatever he put his mind to.

He moves quickly to **Pathos**: the powerful, emotional pull of 'the American Dream' which he presents as under threat from within its borders (the economy) and from outside (war).

It is that promise that has always set this country apart – that through hard work and sacrifice, each of us can pursue our individual dreams but still come together as one American family, to ensure that the next generation can pursue their dreams as well.

That's why I stand here tonight. Because for two hundred and thirty-two years, at each moment when that promise was in jeopardy, ordinary men and women – students and soldiers, farmers and teachers, nurses and janitors – found the courage to keep it alive.

We meet at one of those defining moments – a moment when our nation is at war, our economy is in turmoil, and the American promise has been threatened once more.

This is followed by **Logos**: evidence of the difficulties these threats have led to in the lives of his fellow Americans.

Tonight, more Americans are out of work and more are working harder for less. More of you have lost your homes, and even more are watching your home values plummet. More of you have cars you can't afford to drive, credit card bills you can't afford to pay, and tuition that's beyond your reach.

These challenges are not all of government's making. But the failure to respond is a direct result of a broken politics in Washington and the failed policies of George W. Bush.

His direct attack on George W. Bush's presidency is presented as **Logos**, but he quickly blends this with **Pathos**, speaking of the 'better... more decent... more generous... more compassionate' responses that could be made to the examples of hardship and misery he cites:

America, we are **better** than these last eight years. We are a **better** country than this.

This country is **more decent** than one where a woman in Ohio, on the brink of retirement, finds herself one illness away from disaster after a lifetime of hard work.

This country is **more generous** than one where a man in Indiana has to pack up the equipment he's worked on for twenty years and watch it shipped off to China, and then chokes up as he explains how he felt like a failure when he went home to tell his family the news.

We are **more compassionate** than a government that lets veterans sleep on our streets and families slide into poverty; that sits on its hands while a major American city drowns before our eyes.

Tonight, I say to the American people, to Democrats and Republicans and Independents across this great land – enough! This moment – this election – is our chance to keep, in the twenty-first century, the American promise alive. Because next week, in Minnesota, the same party that brought you two terms of George Bush and Dick Cheney will ask this country for a third. And we are here because we love this country too much to let the next four years look like the last eight. On November 4th, we must stand up and say: 'Eight is enough.'

This is not the whole speech, but the last paragraph here clearly concludes this section, as he returns to the 'American promise' and combines it with his and his party's purpose.

Now let's look at something much older: Elizabeth I's address to her troops at Tilbury, on 9 August 1588:

My loving people,

We have been persuaded by some that are careful of our safety, to take heed how we commit our selves to armed multitudes, for fear of treachery; but I assure you I do not desire to live to distrust my faithful and loving people. Let tyrants fear. I have always so behaved myself that, under God, I have placed my chiefest strength and safeguard in the loyal hearts and good-will of my subjects; and therefore I am come amongst you, as you see, at this time, not for my recreation and disport, but being resolved, in the midst and heat of the battle, to live and die amongst you all; to lay down for my God, and for my kingdom, and my people, my honour and my blood, even in the dust.

I know I have the body of a weak and feeble woman; but I have the heart and stomach of a king, and of a king of England too, and think foul scorn that Parma or Spain, or any prince of Europe, should dare to invade the borders of my realm; to which rather than any dishonour shall grow by me, I myself will take up arms, I myself will be your general, judge, and rewarder of every one of your virtues in the field.

I know already, for your forwardness you have deserved rewards and crowns; and We do assure you on a word of a prince, they shall be duly paid. In the mean time, my lieutenant general shall be in my stead, than whom never prince commanded a more noble or worthy subject; not doubting but by your obedience to my general, by your concord in the camp, and your valour in the field, we shall shortly have a famous victory over these enemies of my God, of my kingdom, and of my people.

Besides writing this and many of her other speeches, Elizabeth was an accomplished poet and her command of rhetoric is evident in this beautiful and powerful speech.

Ethos is clearly important, as she is there to spur on her troops. Her intention, as is appropriate for a pre-battle speech, is to encourage, enthuse and embolden her army for the battle ahead. The first two sections are initially concerned with presenting herself as the embodiment of her kingdom; faithful to God, her people and the common good.

I am come amongst you... to lay down for my God, and for my kingdom, and my people, my honour and my blood, even in the dust.

The most famous sentence in the speech – 'I know I have the body of a weak and feeble woman; but I have the heart and stomach of a king, and of a king of England too' – is a wonderful example of **Ethos**, perfectly appropriate to the context. It also uses **Pathos**, as the language in this figure of speech is passionate and it works at the level of empathy. She wants her understandably fearful men to take courage from her example, by effectively saying, '*I know my body is weak but my determination is strong.*'

She continues with **Pathos**, as she introduces their opponents. She *scorns* those who *dare to invade*, and talks of bravery in battle as *virtues in the field*. She then goes on to speak of *rewards*, and specifically payment for the soldiers: 'you have deserved rewards and crowns; and We do assure you on a word of a prince, they shall be duly paid.' This is another spur to action, but now in the realm of **Logos**: a practical, pragmatic reason to fight well.

Her conclusion brings together the three elements: the well-disciplined and obedient soldier (**Logos**), who fights valiantly for God (**Pathos**) against the enemy of the kingdom (**Ethos**).

Summary

- Rhetoric is the Art of Persuasion.
- Aristotle's three main strategies for persuasion are Ethos, presenting your credentials; Pathos, making people feel something; and Logos, backing up your argument with facts.
- You find these strategies used in speeches made throughout history.
- You will also find these strategies at work in literature, especially in plays.
- Every time you open your mouth on stage you are probably trying to persuade somebody of something.

2.

Rhetoric
in Drama

LOOKING CLOSELY AT A
CHARACTER'S RHETORIC CAN
BE A WAY TO FIND A DEEPER
UNDERSTANDING OF THEIR
NATURE.

The Use of Rhetorical Strategies in Dramatic Speeches

Let's now look at rhetoric in action in a play. *Othello* is a good place to begin and let's look at Othello himself.

Looking closely at a character's rhetoric can be a way to find a deeper understanding of their nature. In the following scene, Othello's use of **Ethos, Pathos** and **Logos** reveals quite a lot about his personal character. There are two sections. First he defends himself against the accusation of Brabantio, his father-in-law, who declares that Othello has 'abused, stolen and corrupted his daughter'. Then he tells him and other Venetian Senators how he won Desdemona's love.

Here are three of his speeches in Act 1, Scene 3:

> OTHELLO. Most potent, grave and reverend signors,
>   My very noble and approved good masters,
>   That I have ta'en away this old man's daughter,
>   It is most true; true I have married her;
>   The very head and front of my offending
>   Hath this extent, no more.

He begins with **Logos**, stating the facts of the situation as they are all agreed upon. Then he moves on to himself; he uses **Ethos**.

>   Rude am I in my speech
>   And little blessed with the soft phrase of peace...
>   And little of this great world can I speak
>   More than pertains to feats of broil and battle:
>   And therefore little shall I grace my cause
>   In speaking for myself.

Then he returns to **Logos** (with a twist of irony).

>   Yet, by your gracious patience,
> I will a round unvarnished tale deliver
> Of my whole course of love: what drugs, what charms,
> What conjuration and what mighty magic –
> For such proceedings I am charged withal –
> I won his daughter.

The next speech is **Ethos**.

> Send for the lady to the Sagittary,
> And let her speak of me before her father.
> If you do find me foul in her report,
> The trust, the office I do hold of you
> Not only take away, but let your sentence
> Even fall upon my life.

And again he sticks to **Ethos**.

> Her father loved me, oft invited me,
> Still questioned me the story of my life
> From year to year – the battles, sieges, fortunes
> That I have passed.
> I ran it through, even from my boyish days
> To th' very moment that he bade me tell it:

Here he moves his storytelling to **Pathos**.

> Wherein I spake of most disastrous chances,
> Of moving accidents by flood and field,
> Of hair-breadth scapes i'th'imminent deadly breach.
> Of being taken by the insolent foe,
> And sold to slavery; of my redemption thence,
> And portance in my travels' history:
> Wherein of antres vast and deserts idle,
> Rough quarries, rocks, and hills whose heads touch
>   heaven,

It was my hint to speak – such was the process:
And of the Cannibals that each other eat,
The Anthropophagi, and men whose heads
Do grow beneath their shoulders.

After the moving précis of his adventures, he returns to the facts with **Logos**.

                    This to hear
Would Desdemona seriously incline:
But still the house affairs would draw her thence,
Which ever as she could with haste dispatch
She'd come again, and with a greedy ear
Devour up my discourse; which I observing
Took once a pliant hour, and found good means
To draw from her a prayer of earnest heart
That I would all my pilgrimage dilate
Whereof by parcels she had something heard,
But not intentively.

Now back to **Pathos** as he presents the picture of the beautiful Desdemona weeping for his past.

               I did consent,
And often did beguile her of her tears
When I did speak of some distressful stroke
That my youth suffered. My story being done,
She gave me for my pains a world of sighs:
She swore, in faith 'twas strange, 'twas passing
                        strange,
'Twas pitiful, 'twas wondrous pitiful;
She wished she had not heard it, yet she wished
That heaven had made her such a man. She thanked
                        me,
And bade me, if I had a friend that loved her,
I should but teach him how to tell my story,
And that would woo her.

He ends with **Logos**; back to the facts.

> Upon this hint I spake:
> She loved me for the dangers I had passed,
> And I loved her, that she did pity them.
> This only is the witchcraft I have used.
> Here comes the lady: let her witness it.

Othello begins with the facts of the matter: **Logos**. But he soon moves on to **Ethos** as he speaks about who he is: reminding the Senators of the wars he has fought on behalf of Venice. He is establishing himself as equal with Brabantio and the Senate in that they all in their own way serve the state. For the actor playing Othello, this could open up some ideas about Othello's sense of self. Is it an indication of a struggle to be treated with the status he deserves? Is he attempting to make his listeners see beyond the difference in race?

As he moves into his personal story, his use of **Ethos** clearly presents his authenticity: as a person of worldly experience; a survivor with the strength of character to support a high-class wife. As he unfolds his story, he is able to introduce **Pathos**, as would the best of storytellers, to move his listeners to empathise with him. And he backs this up, and concludes with **Logos** – facts.

It is a powerful piece of storytelling, and his use of **Ethos**, **Pathos** and **Logos** is successful, at least with the Duke, who says: 'I think this tale would win my daughter too.'

Iago, the arch manipulator, also understands the power of language, but uses rhetoric in much more indirect ways. Let's have a look at this conversation from Act 3, Scene 3, where he is sowing seeds of doubt into Othello's ear.

Iago's **Ethos** is already established in his relationship with Othello. They are veterans who have fought together and placed their trust in each other. However, Iago is of lower rank and he has already told us that the basis for his contempt for Othello is that he promoted his fellow soldier Cassio over him. His use of **Ethos** is set up in the idea that 'Men should be what they seem', which implies that he is just that.

IAGO.   For Michael Cassio,
  I dare be sworn I think that he is honest.

OTHELLO. I think so too.

IAGO.   Men should be what they
                              seem;
  Or those that be not, would they might seem none!

OTHELLO. Certain, men should be what they seem.

IAGO. Why, then, I think Cassio's an honest man.

OTHELLO. Nay, yet there's more in this:
  I prithee speak to me as to thy thinkings,
  As thou dost ruminate, and give thy worst of thoughts
  The worst of words.

Iago sticks with **Ethos** by presenting himself as *dutiful* and a *slave*, but he mixes in a bit of **Logos** as he begins to infect Othello's ear with ideas of man's temptation to sin.

IAGO.   Good my lord, pardon me;
  Though I am bound to every act of duty,
  I am not bound to that all slaves are free to:
  Utter my thoughts. Why, say they are vile and false?
  As where's that palace whereinto foul things
  Sometimes intrude not? Who has a breast so pure,
  But some unclean apprehensions
  Keep leets and law-days, and in session sit
  With meditations lawful?

OTHELLO. Thou dost conspire against thy friend,
Iago,
If thou but think'st him wronged, and mak'st his ear
A stranger to thy thoughts.

Now he knows he's on to something and as Othello is drawn in, Iago returns to **Ethos**, presenting an honest portrait of his nature but in a rather convoluted and disingenuous way. Finally he moves to **Pathos** as he turns the focus of his discourse onto Othello, his prey.

IAGO.   I do beseech you,
Though I perchance am vicious in my guess –
As I confess it is my nature's plague
To spy into abuses, and of my jealousy
Shapes faults that are not – that your wisdom then,
From one that so imperfectly conjects,
Would take no notice, nor build yourself a trouble
Out of his scattering and unsure observance.
It were not for your quiet or your good,
Nor for my manhood, honesty, and wisdom,
To let you know my thoughts.

OTHELLO.   What dost thou mean?

Iago knows his victim well. He now goes straight for the jugular with the introduction of *reputation*. He knows Othello's weakness. He knows that the General has had to strive to gain and maintain the status he deserves within Venetian society.

IAGO. Good name in man and woman, dear my lord,
Is the immediate jewel of their souls.
Who steals my purse, steals trash; 'tis something,
nothing;
'Twas mine, 'tis his, and has been slave to thousands:

> But he that filches from me my good name
> Robs me of that which not enriches him
> And makes me poor indeed.

It is a powerful use of **Pathos**, and it works.

> OTHELLO.   By heaven, I'll know thy thoughts.

Iago continues in the mood of **Pathos**. He has chosen his moment well; Othello is in love and is wide open to his feelings as he revels in his new-found romantic sensibility.

> IAGO. You cannot, if my heart were in your hand,
>   Nor shall not, whilst 'tis in my custody.

> OTHELLO. Ha!

> IAGO.   O, beware, my lord, of jealousy!
>   It is the green-eyed monster, which doth mock
>   The meat it feeds on. That cuckold lives in bliss
>   Who certain of his fate loves not his wronger,
>   But O, what damnèd minutes tells he o'er,
>   Who dotes yet doubts, suspects yet fondly loves!

> OTHELLO. O misery!

> IAGO. Poor and content is rich, and rich enough;
>   But riches fineless is as poor as winter,
>   To him that ever fears he shall be poor.
>   Good God, the souls of all my tribe defend
>   From jealousy!

It is a relentless use of **Pathos** to prepare Othello for the death-blow that is the suggestion that his new wife Desdemona is having an affair with Michael Cassio.

Othello works a great deal from **Ethos**, and it leads to his downfall. His need to be accepted as an equal in Venice makes him vulnerable. Is it pride? Is it longing? Is it a desire for justice? These are the sorts of questions that can arise for the actor playing Othello when they begin to look at his rhetoric.

Iago appears to be always one step ahead and in control of debates, not only with Othello but with Roderigo too. Cassio and Desdemona refer to his honesty but he is less successful with them, and his wife, Emilia, shows how disillusioned she is with him in Act 3, Scene 4.

> EMILIA. 'Tis not a year or two shows us a man:
>   They are all but stomachs, and we all but food;
>   To eat us hungerly, and when they are full,
>   They belch us. Look you, Cassio and my husband!

A colourful and fully felt metaphor.

Playing the Strategies

You may now be thinking: *That's interesting, but what does it mean for an actor? How can I use this?* In the work I do with actors I ask them to play the strategy they have chosen, in the same way they would play an 'action'. Playing actions, as laid out by Max Stafford-Clark in *Letters to George* is the use of a transitive verb to describe and therefore focus the way a character is trying to affect another character or characters they are speaking to: 'I *humour* you', 'I *educate* you' or 'I *seduce* you', for example. By doing so, they are trying to change the other character's thoughts, feelings, actions or behaviour. They are speaking tactically.

Although I am suggesting only three strategies to choose from, the actor should similarly play the strategy actively, in order to change other characters' minds. This shouldn't supersede the 'actioning' technique, but can work well alongside it. For example, if you feel you are playing **Pathos**, you can use actions within that, such as 'I *shame* you', 'I *irritate* you', 'I *hurt* you', 'I *amuse* you'. Within **Ethos** you could use 'I *recruit* you', 'I *reassure* you', 'I *impress* you'. Within **Logos** you could use 'I *enlighten* you', 'I *educate* you', 'I *mislead* you'.

The exercises that follow in this book are designed to help you do this.

Rhetorical Strategies in Dialogue

It is not just in a play's speeches that we see rhetoric at work, but also in dialogue. This is where rhetoric games really come into play, and once recognised can be very useful for actors to find the dynamic of a scene or relationship.

Let's start with something more modern: Arthur Miller's *Death of a Salesman*. In this play there is a constant debate going on, and the debate is about identity. Willy Loman, the travelling salesman of the title, finds himself, in middle age, faced with losing his job. His anxiety and consequential weariness bring up troubling memories from his past that challenge the persona he has tried to present to his family. His existential crisis affects the way he deals with his sons, Happy and Biff, and his wife Linda.

An important element of the play is that his son Biff has returned home from a series of what his father sees as dead-end jobs. This passage from Act 1 is a typical struggle between father and son as to their true identity.

In the dialogue that precedes this section, Happy has suggested that Biff whistling in an elevator had led to him losing a job. Willy refers to Bernard, who is the son of his neighbour, Charley. Bernard is a lawyer and Willy is jealous of the success of this family.

BIFF. Screw the business world!

HAPPY. All right, screw it! Great, but cover yourself!

LINDA. Hap, Hap!

BIFF. I don't care what they think! They've laughed at Dad for years, and you know why? Because we don't belong in this nuthouse of a city! We should be mixing cement on some open plain, or – or carpenters. A carpenter is allowed to whistle!

WILLY *walks in from the entrance of the house, at left.*

WILLY. Even your grandfather was better than a carpenter. You never grew up. Bernard does not whistle in the elevator, I assure you.

BIFF. Yeah, but you do, Pop.

WILLY. I never in my life whistled in an elevator! And who in the business world thinks I'm crazy?

BIFF. I didn't mean it like that, Pop. Now don't make a whole thing out of it, will ya?

WILLY. Go back to the West? Be a carpenter, a cowboy, enjoy yourself!

LINDA. Willy, he was just saying –

WILLY. I heard what he said!

HAPPY. Hey, Pop, come on now…

WILLY. They laugh at me, heh? Go to Filene's, go to the Hub, go to Slattery's, Boston. Call out the name Willy Loman and see what happens! Big shot!

BIFF. All right, Pop.

WILLY. Big!

BIFF. All right!

WILLY. Why do you always insult me?

BIFF. I didn't say a word. Did I say a word?

LINDA. He didn't say anything, Willy.

WILLY. All right, good night, good night.

LINDA. Willy, dear, he just decided...

WILLY. If you get tired hanging around tomorrow, paint the ceiling I put up in the living-room.

BIFF. I'm leaving early tomorrow.

HAPPY. He's going to see Bill Oliver, Pop.

WILLY. Oliver? For what?

BIFF. He always said he'd stake me. I'd like to go into business, so maybe I can take him up on it.

LINDA. Isn't that wonderful?

WILLY. Don't interrupt. What's wonderful about it? There's fifty men in the City of New York who'd stake him. Sporting goods?

BIFF. I guess so. I know something about it and –

WILLY. He knows something about it! You know sporting goods better than Spalding, for God's sake! How much is he giving you?

BIFF. I don't know, I didn't even see him yet, but –

WILLY. Then what're you talkin about?

BIFF. Well, all I said was I'm gonna see him, that's all!

WILLY. Ah, you're counting your chickens again.

BIFF. Oh, Jesus, I'm going to sleep!

Both Willy and Biff are using **Ethos** as their arguments concern their authenticity; who they really are and who they wish the other to be. Biff begins by suggesting they are not really city people and should be labourers or craftsmen working outdoors. Willy's response is that they do not come from what he sees as lowly manual labourers. He tries to shift the argument to their neighbour Bernard, whom he considers to be a good example of the businessman he feels he and his sons should be. But Biff counters by pointing out that he, Biff, is like his father, Willy, who also whistles in elevators. Here he uses **Logos** as he is stating a fact, but it could also be played using **Pathos** as he is trying to lift his father's mood with this affectionate remark. If you are playing this role, you could try both to see which feels right.

Willy does not choose to hear this affection, and counters with what he considers to be **Logos**: the fact that he never whistles in elevators. He then demands facts from his son; to name who said he's crazy, harking back to an earlier remark he's overheard but which did not refer to him. In this speech, however, he is also now moving to **Pathos**, throwing emotional challenges at his family and raising the temperature of the debate. This is a choice he usually makes when he feels he is losing control of an argument or not achieving the degree of respect he feels he is owed. The other members of the family quickly find themselves drawn into the same mood, although Biff tries to calm the situation by agreeing with him – a strategy that doesn't work.

Happy also chooses to placate his father by following his father's preferred conversational practice of looking for good news (**Pathos**). He tells him that Biff is going to see an old employer to ask for a business loan. Willy jumps on this and begins to fantasise, using **Hyperbole** in an attempt to back up his argument: 'There's fifty men in the City of New York who'd stake him' and 'You know sporting goods better than Spalding, for God's sake!' – both false **Logos**.

The use of **Hyperbole**, or exaggeration, can be an effective part of a rhetorical strategy. Here, Willy is using it to bolster what he wants to present as facts, but it is of course a use of **Pathos**, as his main aim is to make his sons and himself feel important. He maintains the drive of the argument by twice cutting off his sons' replies to his questions. He allows himself to develop the fantasy, not giving Biff the chance to explain the truth of the situation.

Happy and Linda unsuccessfully try to control Willy by switching with him as he veers through the extremes of rhetoric. We see later in the play that Happy has become a chip off the old block by also using false **Logos**, exaggerating his achievements at work.

So we see Biff, Willy and Happy using **Ethos**, **Pathos** and **Logos** to try to persuade the others of their point of view.

The Exercises

After each of the rhetorical elements I introduce you to in this book, I will offer you some exercises to help you identify and then actively use the element. You could try them out with the texts I have explored or with the play you are working on. I will also suggest other plays where you can find that particular trope.

Here are some exercises designed to unlock the rhetorical strategies of **Ethos**, **Pathos** and **Logos**.

Exercise 1

Speak or read your text aloud. Section by section, decide if you are using one of these strategies. Say the name of the strategy before you speak that section.

Let me remind you of the action you are playing in these three strategies:

Ethos: This is who I am; you know me, you can trust me; I've had experience with the thing I'm talking about.

Pathos: I want you to feel something; to be moved.

Logos: Here are the reasons you should believe me; the facts, the evidence.

By naming the strategy first, you will find you use the element strongly as you speak the line. It will also help you to confirm your choice or change your mind.

Speak the text again without saying the name of the elements you are using. Can you still feel the strategy at work?

If you feel you can't decide which strategy the character is using at any given point, try using a different one to see how it feels. Read or listen to the responses of the other characters in the scene. Recognising how they respond can help you be clear about your character's tactic.

Exercise 2

'I am, you feel, I know.'

If **Ethos, Pathos** and **Logos** seem a bit daunting, you could try making them more personal.

Have another go at speaking your text and this time, if you think a piece of your character's speech is about who they are, before you speak it, say 'I am'. When you say that, make it as true and real as you can and see if it has an effect on the lines of text. Does it help you to own the thought? Does it say something about your authenticity, your **Ethos**?

If you think the character is trying to make their listeners feel something, try saying 'you feel', and then name what you are trying to make them feel (shame, or happiness, or worry, for example) before that piece of text. Does this help you to focus on shifting their feelings? Can you use this **Pathos** persuasively?

If you think your character is laying out facts, or evidence, then say 'I know' before you speak the text. Does this help you to begin to convey a sense of conviction about the evidence you are laying out? Are you using **Logos** actively?

Speak the text again without 'I am, you feel, I know'. Can you retain the strategies? Are they effective?

Exercise 3

Now try focusing on the elements in a physical way. Speak or read your text and do the following actions according to which strategy you think you are using:

Ethos: Raise your hand.

Pathos: Put your hand on your heart, or if you are working with another actor or actors, put it on the heart of the person you are speaking to.

Logos: Put your hand on your head. Or on the head of your listener.

Then speak your text again without the physical actions. Be aware of the choices you are making.

You could make decisions first and mark on your script which sections are which, to remind you of how your character is choosing to use their language.

Exercise 4

In the spring of 2017 we began rehearsals for *Twelfth Night* directed by Simon Godwin for the Olivier Theatre. After teaching the acting company about these strategies I set up the following exercise which you could adapt for your play and your actors.

I divided the company into three groups. The task for each group was to prepare a persuasive speech for one of them to speak. They were to persuade Simon to fall in love with them. Each group had to use a different strategy with which to persuade: one group using **Ethos**, one using **Pathos** and one, **Logos**. I gave them about twenty minutes to write and prepare before one of them addressed Simon. He finally chose the one who won him over. Can you guess which one?

You will find you can use these exercises with many texts. Here are a few suggestions.

Seán O'Casey, *Juno and the Paycock*. It is interesting to consider how characters use or favour one of the strategies generally, but in Act 3, telling of Mary's pregnancy, they really come into play.

Caryl Churchill, *Top Girls*, Act 2, Scene 4, Mrs Kidd and Marlene.

Harold Pinter, *The Homecoming*. An interesting text to consider for the use of these strategies throughout.

Shakespeare, *Antony and Cleopatra*. There is plenty of persuasion going on in this play with characters using or favouring particular strategies.

You will find these exercises particularly useful with the classical Greek canon of plays, whose authors of course use all these strategies; *Medea*, *Antigone*, *The Women of Troy*, the *Oedipus* plays, to name but a few.

Summary

- Characters in a play will often use different strategies in order to persuade other characters – or in the case of a soliloquy, themselves – of something.
- Rhetorical strategies can be found in both a play's speeches and its dialogue.
- Remember to play your chosen strategy actively.
- Physicalising your actions, as an exercise, can help you to make them clear.
- Identifying your character's use of strategies can reveal things about their nature.

3.

Other Rhetorical Strategies in Drama

EVERY TIME YOU OPEN YOUR
MOUTH ON STAGE YOU
ARE TRYING TO PERSUADE
SOMEBODY OF SOMETHING.

Aristotle was concerned with the concept that arguments have to be 'found' and that it requires art to do so. Within dialogue, there are various ways that argument can be found.

Appropriating Your Opponent's Vocabulary

In my imagined Planning Meeting I showed you how you can find your argument from within that of your opponent.

I pointed out that a very powerful rhetorical device is to use a word, phrase or image that your opponent has used and turn it to your advantage. By doing so you can subvert or sabotage their argument by adopting the vocabulary or language they have used and changing its meaning. Sometimes just one word is used to change the balance of an argument. This can be a very successful way to take control of an argument and we often see it in action in plays.

In this passage from *Death of a Salesman* there is an example of this:

LINDA. Isn't that **wonderful**?

WILLY. Don't interrupt. What's **wonderful about it**! There's fifty men in the City of New York who'd stake him. Sporting goods?

BIFF. I guess so. **I know something about it** and –

WILLY. **He knows something about it! You know sporting goods better than Spalding, for God's sake!** How much is he giving you!

In this instance Willy is practically taking the words out of his son's mouth. He doesn't let him finish what he's saying and leaps on his words, taking over the debate.

However, he is not using the device successfully. He undermines it by once again stopping his son from making his own point. He is also using it within the context of his usual exaggeration and fantasy. Biff is too familiar with this habit to be persuaded.

An example of the device being used successfully is found in Act 3 of Henrik Ibsen's *A Doll's House* as translated by Michael Meyer. Mrs Linde, a widow, and Nils Krogstad were in love when they were young but financial need led Mrs Linde to marry someone else. Many years later they have met again.

> MRS LINDE. I've **learned** to look at things practically. **Life** and poverty have **taught me** that.
>
> KROGSTAD. And **life has taught me** to distrust fine words.
>
> MRS LINDE. **Then it has taught you a useful lesson.** But surely you still believe in actions?
>
> KROGSTAD. What do you mean?
>
> MRS LINDE. You said you were **like a shipwrecked man clinging to a spar.**
>
> KROGSTAD. I have good reason to say it.
>
> MRS LINDE. I'm in the same position as you. No one to care about, no one to care for.
>
> KROGSTAD. You made **your own choice**.
>
> MRS LINDE. **I had no choice – then.**

KROGSTAD. Well?

MRS LINDE. Nils, suppose **we two shipwrecked souls could join hands**?

KROGSTAD. What are you saying?

MRS LINDE. **Castaways** have a better chance of survival together than on their own.

Krogstad tries to take control of the argument by picking up and distorting her words 'life', 'learned', 'taught', but she takes them back and uses them to draw him closer to her by agreeing with him. Next she takes over the word-stealing device when he talks about 'choice'. She then refers back to the shipwrecked simile he has used a few lines earlier and turns it into an extended metaphor to describe her view of their potential future. Using Krogstad's own simile should be a very effective way to impress an idea on his mind. Mrs Linde is definitely in the driving seat in this particular debate and in the end succeeds in winning Krogstad to her point of view.

Let's have a look at an example found in a much older play. In Act 1, Scene 4 of Christopher Marlowe's *Edward II* the powerful noblemen try to persuade King Edward to give up his relationship with his favourite, Pierce Gaveston, a man of lowly status. They wish to have him banished. Here too, characters repeat words and images used by others and change them to their advantage.

Enter LANCASTER, WARWICK, PEMBROKE, *the* ELDER MORTIMER, YOUNG MORTIMER, THE ARCHBISHOP OF CANTERBURY *and* ATTENDANTS.

LAN. Here is the form of Gaveston's exile:
  May it please your lordship to subscribe your name.

A. OF CANT. Give me the paper.

He subscribes, as do the others after him.

LAN. Quick, quick, my lord; I long to write my name.   4

WAR. But I long more to see him banished hence.

Y. MOR. The name of Mortimer shall fright the king,
Unless he be declined from that base peasant.

Enter KING EDWARD, GAVESTON, *and* KENT.

K. EDW. What, are you moved that Gaveston sits
                              here?   8
It is our pleasure; we will have it so.

LAN. Your grace doth well to place him by your side,
For nowhere else the new earl is so safe.

E. MOR. What man of noble birth can brook this
                             sight? 12
Quam male conveniunt!
See what a scornful look the peasant casts!

PEM. Can kingly lions fawn on creeping ants?

WAR. Ignoble vassal, that like Phaeton   16
Aspir'st unto the guidance of the sun!

Y. MOR. Their downfall is at hand, their forces down;
We will not thus be faced and over-peered.

K. EDW. Lay hands on that traitor Mortimer!   20

E. MOR. Lay hands on that traitor Gaveston!

KENT. Is this the duty that you owe your king?

WAR. We know our duties – let him know his peers.

K. EDW. Whither will you bear him? Stay, or ye shall die.

E. MOR. We are no traitors; therefore threaten not.

GAV. No, threaten not, my lord, but pay them home!
  Were I a king –

Y. MOR. Thou villain, wherefore talk'st thou of a king, 28
  That hardly art a gentleman by birth?

K. EDW. Were he a peasant, being my minion,
  I'll make the proudest of you stoop to him.

LAN. My lord, you may not thus disparage us.– 32
  Away, I say, with hateful Gaveston!

E. MOR. And with the Earl of Kent that favours him.

ATTENDANTS *remove* KENT *and* GAVESTON.

K. EDW. Nay, then, lay violent hands upon your king.
  Here, Mortimer, sit thou in Edward's throne; 36
  Warwick and Lancaster, wear you my crown.
  Was ever king thus over-ruled as I?

LAN. Learn then to rule us better, and the realm.

Y. MOR. What we have done, our heart-blood shall
                                      maintain. 40

WAR. Think you that we can brook this upstart pride?

K. EDW. Anger and wrathful fury stops my speech.

A. OF CANT. Why are you moved? Be patient, my lord,
  And see what we your counsellors have done. 44

Y. MOR. My lords, now let us all be resolute,
  And either have our wills, or lose our lives.

K. EDW. Meet you for this, proud overbearing peers?
  Ere my sweet Gaveston shall part from me, 48
  This isle shall fleet upon the ocean,
  And wander to the unfrequented Ind.

A. OF CANT. You know that I am legate to the Pope.
On your allegiance to the see of Rome,   52
Subscribe, as we have done, to his exile.

Y. MOR. Curse him, if he refuse; and then may we
Depose him and elect another king.

K. EDW. Ay, there it goes! but yet I will not yield.   56
Curse me, depose me, do the worst you can.

LAN. Then linger not, my lord, but do it straight.

A. OF CANT. Remember how the bishop was abused!
Either banish him that was the cause thereof,   60
Or I will presently discharge these lords
Of duty and allegiance due to thee.

K. EDW (*Aside*). It boots me not to threat; I must speak
                                                   fair. –
The legate of the Pope will be obeyed.   64
My lord, you shall be Chancellor of the realm;
Thou, Lancaster, High Admiral of our fleet;
Young Mortimer and his uncle shall be earls;
And you, Lord Warwick, President of the North;   68
And thou, of Wales. If this content you not,
Make several kingdoms of this monarchy,
And share it equally amongst you all,
So I may have some nook or corner left,   72
To frolic with my dearest Gaveston.

A. OF CANT. Nothing shall alter us, we are resolved.

LAN. Come, come, subscribe.

Y. MOR. Why should you love him whom the world
                                           hates so? 76

K. EDW. Because he loves me more than all the world.

Ah, none but rude and savage-minded men
Would seek the ruin of my Gaveston;
You that be noble-born should pity him.   80

WAR. You that are princely-born should shake him off.
For shame subscribe, and let the lown depart.

E. MOR. Urge him, my lord.

A. OF CANT. Are you content to banish him the
realm? 84

K. EDW. I see I must, and therefore am content.
Instead of ink, I'll write it with my tears. [*Subscribes.*]

There are many occasions in this argument when one speaker picks up the word, phrase or image that another has used and then turns it to support their own argument, or to emphasise strong commitment to their own beliefs. At the beginning of the scene, before King Edward arrives, the nobles speak of the document they have prepared to order the banishment of Gaveston, the King's favourite companion. They are competing with each other to show their eagerness to sign it and rid the court of Gaveston. Lancaster declares 'I **long** to write my name', followed by Warwick's 'But **I long more** to see him banished'. Later on, when swords are drawn, Kent, who is loyal to Edward, asks 'Is this the **duty** that you owe your king?' Warwick answers '*We know* our duties – let *him know* his peers'. By responding in this way, using Warwick's words, he counters Kent's attempt to remind them of their duty, by reminding him that it works both ways; implying that rule is maintained by the agreement of all to adhere to accepted power structures. It is a concise response.

This argument concerning hierarchy has already been established in the exchange above, when the nobles pick up on Mortimer Senior's description of Gaveston as a peasant. The argument is first developed by Pembroke using the metaphor of lions and ants. It is then taken up by Warwick and Mortimer Junior in the simile that compares Gaveston's ambition to Phaethon wanting to be as powerful as his father the sun and who, by reaching too high, brought about his own downfall. Edward, later on, throws their argument back to them. He picks up their word 'peasant' and says that through his power he will make the nobles 'stoop' to Gaveston.

> Were he a **peasant**, being my minion,
> I'll make the proudest of you **stoop to him**.

The word-grabbing continues in the next exchange. Edward complains,

> Was ever king thus **overruled** as I?

To which Lancaster responds,

> Learn then to **rule us better** and the realm.

Then again at lines 76 and 77,

> YOUNG MORTIMER. Why should **you love him whom the world hates so**?

> EDWARD. Because **he loves me more than all the world.**

And lines 80, 81 and 82,

> EDWARD. You that be **noble-born** should **pity him.**

> WARWICK. You that are **princely-born** should **shake him off.**

Exercise 5

This exercise uses physical objects to represent the words or phrases that are being used in the debate. If you use a text where there are only two speakers, each should have an equal number of marbles, pencils, books, balls or some other objects that can be easily moved. If you are using the *Edward II* text or another with more than one participant, then decide how many sides there are to the argument and each side should have some objects.

Read or speak the text and whenever someone repeats or uses another person's word, phrase or image, that person takes one of their opponents' objects *as they repeat the words*. It is important that the speaker picks up the object as they speak the words. By doing so they make the words solid, tangible things that are being powerfully manipulated. At the end of the scene you can see who has the most objects.

Read or speak the text again without the objects but with the memory of what they taught you about the way the speakers are working the language to gain what they want.

Exercise 6

If you are in a room where there are plenty of chairs and/or other small furniture, you could create a furniture sculpture of each part of your argument; placing the pieces on top of and around each other.

If one person is taking on the argument of the other, they could create their own sculpture from that of their opponent. If they use just one word, they could just take one piece of furniture.

You could even do this exercise with the contents of a bag or pencil case.

Then read or speak the text again with the memory of the exercise.

Exercise 7

This exercise moves you on from the word-grabbing technique to discover how well each side performs generally in the debate. It is a good exercise to try when there are more actors present than there are in the scene.

Again decide on the number of sides to the argument and then assign some people who are not in the scene to each side. They will act as supporters or cheerleaders to their speaker or speakers.

Read or speak the scene and whenever the supporters feel their side is making a good argument they should cheer or clap. They should not be drowning out the speaker but encouraging them on. They need to listen carefully and respond precisely to what they are hearing; to the language of the argument.

Read or speak the text again without the supporters but with the memory of how they encouraged good argument. How they responded to specific words or phrases.

You could also take the exercise further and allow the supporters to boo the opposing team. Again make sure this is in response to close listening and not too enthusiastic. It can make speakers use their words, and therefore their argument, with more muscularity and conviction.

Summary

- Look for or listen for when characters choose to take a word or phrase from their opponent's argument and use it in their own.
- This is a strong rhetorical device that enables the speaker to take control of an argument or debate.
- It can reduce the power of the other person's argument and force them to find new avenues to pursue.
- Use exercises to strengthen each character's use of the language they are given to argue or debate.

These types of exercises can make the argument clear for you; helping you to own and embody the language and ideas.

Revealing the Themes of the Play

In the scene we looked at from *Death of a Salesman*, we began to see that by exploring the way characters use rhetoric, actors can uncover the deep themes of the play and therefore the deep motivations of each character. In that play, we see how social change can affect an individual's sense of identity; how modern life can bear upon the individual's self-worth and their coping strategies.

By using the rhetorical strategies powerfully, actors can make these clear to the audience, so that storytelling and characterisations work hand in hand.

Let's now look at Act 1, Scene 2 of *A Raisin in the Sun*, written by Lorraine Hansberry and first produced in 1959.

The play is set in Chicago in an African American household. Walter's mother, Mama, a widow, is expecting to receive the money from her late husband's life-insurance policy in the mail today. Some of the money is to be put aside to send Walter's sister, Beneatha, to medical school. Walter doesn't know what his mother intends to do with the rest but he hopes she will give it to him to invest in a liquor store he wants to open with two friends. Ruth is Walter's wife.

WALTER. Did it come?

MAMA. Can't you give people a Christian greeting before you start asking about money?

WALTER. Did it come?

RUTH *unfolds the cheque and lays it quietly before him, watching him intently with thoughts of her own.* WALTER *sits down and grasps it close and counts off the zeros.*

Ten thousand dollars.

He turns suddenly, frantically to his mother and draws some papers out of his breast pocket.

Mama – look. Old Willy Harris put everything on paper –

MAMA. Son – I think you ought to talk to your wife… I'll go on out and leave you alone if you want –

WALTER. I can talk to her later. Mama, look –

MAMA. Son –

WALTER. WILL SOMEBODY PLEASE LISTEN TO ME TODAY!

MAMA. I don't 'low no yellin' in this house, Walter

Lee, and you know it – And there ain't going to be no investing in no liquor stores.

WALTER. But, Mama, you ain't even looked at it.

MAMA. I don't aim to have to speak on that again.

Long pause.

WALTER. You ain't looked at it and you don't aim to have to speak on that again? You ain't even looked at it and you decided – Well, *you* tell that to my boy tonight when you put him to sleep on the living-room couch! [...]

RUTH. Where are you going?

WALTER. I'm going out!

RUTH. Where?

WALTER. Just out of this house somewhere –

RUTH. I'll come too.

WALTER. I don't want you to come!

RUTH. I got something to talk to you about, Walter.

WALTER. That's too bad.

MAMA. Walter Lee – Sit down!

WALTER. I'm a grown man, Mama.

MAMA. Ain't nobody said you wasn't grown. But you still in my house and my presence. And as long as you are – you'll talk to your wife civil. Now sit down.

RUTH. Oh, let him go on out and drink himself to death! He makes me sick to my stomach!

RUTH *goes into the bedroom and slams the door.*

WALTER. And you turn mine too, baby! That was my biggest mistake –

MAMA. Walter, what is the matter with you?

WALTER. Matter with me? Ain't nothing the matter with *me*!

MAMA. Yes, there is. Something eating you up like a crazy man. Something more than me not giving you this money. The past few years I been watching it happen to you. You get all nervous acting and kind of wild in the eyes – I said sit there now, I'm talking to you!

WALTER. Mama – I don't need no nagging at me today.

MAMA. Seem like you getting to a place where you always tied up in some kind of knot about something. But if anybody ask you 'bout it you just yell at 'em and bust out the house and go out and drink somewheres. Walter Lee, people can't live with that. Ruth's a good, patient girl in her way – but you getting to be too much. Boy, don't make the mistake of driving that girl away from you.

WALTER. Why – what she ever do for me?

MAMA. She loves you.

In this section, the debate between Walter and his mother plays out one of the main themes of the play: the juggling of roles and status within an extended family living in one house. These relationships are constrained by the family's financial situation. Their poverty not only dictates their living conditions but also the extent of their ambitions. Both Mama and Walter see power as residing in whoever has money or property and they both often favour **Ethos** in their arguments. But emotions are near the surface at this time in this family, so **Pathos** is also often called upon.

Although we know Walter is excited by the prospect of the insurance cheque, he tries to begin his persuasive tactics calmly and rationally. He uses **Logos** as he attempts to show his mother the figures his friend Willy has prepared. Her response is to take control of the conversation by ignoring what he has said and redirecting him to what she wants him to do. At the same time trying to avoid the subject he wants to discuss.

Walter's emotions easily take over as he shouts to be noticed, but his mother continues to block him and uses **Ethos** to back up her stance, 'I don't 'low no yellin' in this house, Walter Lee, and you know it.' The argument then centres on the house, Mama's ownership of it and its inadequate size for their family.

Walter clings to **Logos**, determinedly trying to set up an argument, but then switches to the ace in his **Pathos** pack and brings his son into play: 'Well, *you* tell that to my boy tonight when you put him to sleep on the living-room couch!'

Once Ruth has entered the conversation Mama finds another opportunity to reinforce her status with **Ethos** – 'you still in my house and my presence'. She expects him to listen to her when she has pointedly ignored his words at the beginning of the scene.

Talking and listening are central to their exchanges and simply following the track of how they use words relating to this can give the actors a clear sense of the core of the conflict – not just of this debate but of the whole play. Being listened to implies the acknowledgement of some sort of status: the status that Mama and Walter cannot achieve in American society at this time. And when they can't find it in the world, they need to find it at home, at least. Who is being listened to matters. The shifting uses of 'yell', 'speak', 'talk', 'nag' can also be tactical as each tries to control the argument and maintain their status.

We have already seen Mama's refusal to respond to Walter's words at the beginning of the scene and his outburst:

WILL SOMEBODY PLEASE **LISTEN TO ME** TODAY!

Mama tells him off for 'yellin'' and referring to the proposed liquor store says,

I don't aim to have **to speak on that** again.

Which Walter takes hold of and repeats, sarcastically taking it into his own argument.

You ain't looked at it and you don't aim to have **to speak on that** again?

Ruth needs him to listen to her:

I got something **to talk to you** about, Walter.

But he doesn't want to listen to her right now and repels her harshly.

His mother's response to that is:

But you still in my house and my presence. And as long as you are – you'll **talk to your wife civil**.

When his reply is dismissive of both his mother and his wife and he doesn't want to hear what Mama is saying, she pushes him to listen:

I said sit there now, **I'm talking to you**!

He diminishes her argument by reinterpreting her word 'talking' with his reply:

Mama – I don't need no **nagging at me** today.

Then ironically, considering her refusal to listen to him at the start of the scene, Mama accuses him of not listening when he is questioned about his state of mind:

But if anybody **ask** you 'bout it you just **yell** at 'em.

After this they do finally have a conversation.

The two sides of the argument in the next section show the difference of experience between the two generations. We hear that Mama's deep concerns are for her family to stay safe, whereas Walter is desperate to stretch his wings and prove himself in the cut and thrust of the modern commercial world. They have different ideas of freedom. His life has been lived in the urban, fast-moving, Northern city. Mama's defining experiences were in the segregated, brutal, rural, Southern states. These points of view are established in the first exchange:

WALTER (*a beat*). Mama – I'm going out. I want to go off somewhere and be by myself for a while.

MAMA. I'm sorry 'bout your liquor store, son. It just wasn't the right thing for us to do. That's what I want to tell you about –

WALTER. I got to go out, Mama –

MAMA. **It's dangerous**, son.

WALTER. **What's dangerous**?

MAMA. When a man **goes outside his home** to look for peace.

WALTER. Then why can't there never be **no peace in this house**, then?

We would hear from Mama's 'It's dangerous' that she thinks it's dangerous outside. But she's concerned with more than physical safety. She's talking about *peace*, which for her is found at home with the gratitude of what you have there; a private, safe family space of your own. Walter says he wants peace too, but we know he cannot find that in the way things stand in his home: 'I want so many things…'

As the conversation continues:

MAMA. You done found it **in some other house**?

WALTER. No – there ain't no woman! Why do women always think there's a woman somewhere when a man gets restless? Do you know what this money means to me? Do you know what this money can do for us? Mama – Mama – I want so many things…

MAMA. Yes, son –

WALTER. I want so many things that they are driving me kind of crazy… Mama – **look at me**.

MAMA. **I'm looking at you**. You a good-looking boy. You got **a job**, a nice wife, a fine boy and –

WALTER. **A job. Mama, a job**? I open and close car doors all day long. I drive a man around in his limousine and say, 'Yes, sir,' 'No, sir,' 'Very good, sir,' 'Shall I take the drive, sir?' Mama, that ain't no kind of a job… that ain't nothin' at all. Mama, I don't know if I can **make you understand**.

Mama's idea of safety ('You got a job, a nice wife, a fine boy and –') seems to Walter to be the bare minimum of subsistence and still a form of slavery ('"Yes, sir," "No, sir,"

"Very good, sir."'). For Walter, the only kind of freedom he wants comes with money, and in the next exchange they clearly describe their different views of safety and freedom.

MAMA. **Understand what**, baby?

WALTER. Sometimes it's like I can see the future stretched out in front of me – just plain as day. The future, Mama. Hanging over there at the edge of my days. Just waiting for me – a big, looming blank space – full of *nothing*.

Just waiting for *me*. But it don't have to be. Mama – sometimes when I'm downtown [driving that man around] and I pass them cool, quiet-looking restaurants where them white boys are sitting back and talking 'bout things… sitting there turning deals worth millions of dollars… sometimes I see guys don't look much older than me –

MAMA. Son – how come you **talk so much 'bout money**?

WALTER. Because **it is life**, Mama!

MAMA. Oh – So now it's life. **Money is life**. Once upon a time **freedom used to be life – now it's money**. I guess the world really do change…

WALTER. No – it was always money, Mama. We just didn't know about it.

MAMA. No… something has changed. You something new, boy. In my time we was worried about not being lynched and getting to the North if we could and how to stay alive and still have a pinch of dignity too… Now here come you and Beneatha – talking 'bout things we ain't never even thought about hardly, me and your daddy. You ain't satisfied or proud of nothing we done. I mean that you had a home; that we kept you out of trouble till you was grown; that you don't have to ride to work on back of nobody's streetcar – You my children – but how different we done become.

WALTER. You don't understand, Mama, you just don't understand.

And Mama's right, Walter is 'something new'.

In *A Raisin in the Sun*, Walter and Mama know that listening is important but it's not until the end of the section that they really hear each other, even though they may not quite understand the other's point of view.

Exercise 8

This is a version of Exercise 5. This time you give your objects to others rather than take theirs.

Have to hand a collection of small objects. They could be pens and pencils, cups, cutlery or the contents of your bag; any things that are small enough to handle easily. Each character should have their own collection.

As you read the dialogue, whenever you speak something that feels challenging or is a provocation to the other person, hand them an object or objects from your collection as you speak the words. If the person being given the object then replies with the same words or idea, they should hand the object back as they speak the words. If you think the dialogue warrants it, one character could throw an object (if it is a soft object) to or at the other character.

With the extract above, you could pass or take the objects on the words and phrases I have marked in bold.

Then repeat the dialogue without the objects but with the memory of handing over or throwing tangible things.

You could also try this exercise with chairs or even tables. You could then choose to pick up or move something bigger if you feel the idea or issue you raise is big enough in your world to warrant a big physical object.

Summary

- The main themes of a play are often revealed when you rigorously explore the language and strategies used by both sides in a debate or conflict.
- This rigorous examination will help you to get under the skin of your character.
- It will also help you to speak their choice of language clearly and effectively.

Here are some other texts where you could explore the appropriation of language in dialogue with these exercises, where the information or ideas are being challenged, debated or exchanged:

Helen Edmundson's adaptation of Andrea Levy's *Small Island*, Act 2, Scene 7, Bernard and Gilbert. Chairs and tables are good for this scene.

Timberlake Wertenbaker, *Our Country's Good*, Act 1, Scene 7 ('Harry and Duckling Go Rowing').

Simon Stephens' adaptation of Mark Haddon's *The Curious Incident of the Dog in the Night-Time*, Scene 18, The Street, Mrs Alexander and Christopher.

Lee Hall, *The Pitman Painters*: what is art? What is good painting?

Shakespeare, *Measure for Measure*, Act 3, Scene 1, Angelo and Isabella debating virginity v. death.

Shakespeare, *A Midsummer Night's Dream*, Act 1, Scene 1, Helena and Hermia; Act 3, Scene 2, Helena, Hermia, Lysander and Demetrius.

Githa Sowerby, *Rutherford and Son*, all the scenes between Rutherford and his children, Dick, John and Janet.

Dislocation

There are other ways that characters can try to gain ground in their life through speech. One of these in dialogue is to dislocate what might be the accepted hierarchical structure within the society they are part of.

Normal conversation involves taking it in turns to speak, and the language used will reflect the relative status of the people speaking; those of lower status perhaps giving way to those of higher status, or using politeness. For example, if a request is made or an instruction given, it would normally be made more indirectly by a lower-status person: 'Would you mind closing the door?' as opposed to 'Shut the door please.'

However, this convention could be broken in an attempt to challenge or undermine a person with higher status or influence. We've already seen it in *Edward II* as the nobles challenge Edward's judgement and ability to rule.

In J. B. Priestley's *An Inspector Calls*, we witness a very interesting series of status challenges.

At the beginning of Act 1, a comfortable, middle-class family is celebrating the engagement of their daughter.

The evening is interrupted by the Inspector who brings news and questions. Mr Birling, the senior member of the Birling family, doesn't like being questioned. As a successful businessman he is used to being listened to and having his opinion taken as authority. We see him striving to take control of the conversation which is being led by the Inspector.

Open and Closed Questions

The power struggle is in part played out through the use of questions. In particular, open and closed questions. A closed question is one that allows only a short answer, often just a 'yes' or 'no':

— You did steal the money, didn't you?

— What time did you say you left the house?

It is usually used in an attempt to close down conversation and debate. It can also be used to present opinion or theses as inarguable fact:

Everyone thinks that football team is the best in the world because they have the best coach. Isn't that right?

An open question invites conversation and opinion and therefore a longer reply:

Why do you think that football team is the best in the world?

In this section of the scene, the Inspector has just told the family that a young woman, who had formally been in Birling's employ, has taken her own life by drinking bleach. Mr Birling's son Eric is also part of the conversation. Birling recollects that the young woman had taken part in a strike at his factory.

BIRLING. Look – there's nothing mysterious – or scandalous – about this business – at least not so far as I'm concerned. It's a perfectly straightforward case, and as it happened more than eighteen months ago – nearly two years ago – **obviously it has nothing whatever to do with the wretched girl's suicide. Eh, Inspector?**

Birling's tone is firm and affirmative and he tries to keep control of the situation by asking a closed question which he invites the Inspector to agree with. But the Inspector doesn't agree, which Birling immediately challenges.

INSPECTOR. No, sir. I can't agree with you there.

BIRLING. Why not?

INSPECTOR. Because what happened to her then may have determined what happened to her afterwards, and what happened to her afterwards may have driven her to suicide. A chain of events.

The Inspector's tone is more cautious; he uses 'may have' rather than Birling's 'it is, it has'.

Birling continues in his confident and dismissive way. He again uses a closed question but doesn't realise its implications.

BIRLING. Oh well – put like that, there's something in what you say. Still, I can't accept any responsibility. **If we were all responsible for everything that happened to everybody we'd had anything to do with, it would be very awkward, wouldn't it?**

INSPECTOR. Very awkward.

BIRLING. We'd all be in an impossible position, wouldn't we?

ERIC. By Jove, yes. And as you were saying, Dad, a man has to look after himself –

BIRLING. Yes, well, we needn't go into all that.

INSPECTOR. **Go into what?**

The Inspector's question is an open one and Birling enjoys the invitation to explain. Not realising where it will lead.

BIRLING. Oh – just before you came – I'd been giving these young men a little good advice. Now – about this girl, Eva Smith. I remember her quite well now. She was a lively good-looking girl – country-bred, I fancy – and she'd been working in one of our machine shops for over a year. A good worker too. In fact, the foreman there told me he was ready to promote her into what we call a leading operator – head of a small group of girls. But after they came back from their holidays that August, they were all rather restless, and they suddenly decided to ask for more money. They were averaging about twenty-two and six, which was neither more nor less than is paid generally in our industry. They wanted the rates raised so that they could average about twenty-five shillings a week. I refused, of course.

After this explanation, the Inspector continues to challenge him by asking a simple, open question. The apparent simplicity of these questions is a strong challenge to Birling's assumed authority, and he doesn't like it.

INSPECTOR. **Why?**

BIRLING. Did you say 'Why?'?

INSPECTOR. **Yes. Why did you refuse?**

BIRLING. Well, Inspector, I don't see that it's any concern of yours how I choose to run my business. Is it now?

Birling tries to regain control by not answering the question. Instead, he attempts to counter the challenge by asking a question of his own. This is another closed question, one not requiring an answer; a statement of fact rather than an open question. But the Inspector answers it.

INSPECTOR. It might be, you know.

BIRLING. I don't like the tone.

INSPECTOR. I'm sorry. **But you asked me a question.**

BIRLING. **And you asked me a question before that**, a quite unnecessary question too.

INSPECTOR. **It's my duty to ask questions.**

See how they both wrestle over control of the conversation using that one important word 'question'. Who has the right to ask questions and expect them to be answered?

Now 'duty' becomes the operative word. A word that both are using to support their status.

BIRLING. **Well, it's my duty to keep labour costs down,** and if I'd agreed to this demand for a new rate we'd have added about twelve per cent to our labour costs. Does that satisfy you? So I refused. Said I couldn't consider it. We were paying the usual rates and if they didn't like those rates, they could go and work somewhere else. It's a free country, I told them.

ERIC. It isn't if you can't go and work somewhere else.

INSPECTOR. Quite so.

BIRLING (*to* ERIC). Look – just you keep out of this.

Birling's confidence means he likes the sound of his own voice and he is easily led into condemning himself. The Inspector is the opposite and his syntax is economical and direct. But his real strength in interrogating the Birlings is that he listens carefully. We will come to listening later on in the book.

Exercise 9

This is to explore open and closed questions.

If you are in the scene, go and stand near the door to the room in which you are working. You will have to decide whether the door is open or closed before you begin. Whenever a character asks a closed question, they should shut the door as they ask it. Whenever a character asks an open question, they should open the door as they ask.

Clearly you all need to be on the same side of the door or you may find yourself trying to shout the scene through a closed door!

Repeat the scene without the door opening and closing. Can you invest the scene with the memory of those physical actions?

You could develop this exercise to include any sort of shutting down of argument or of trying to shut out other characters' involvement in a debate.

Exercise 10

This time, if you think you are asking a closed question, walk away from the person or people you are talking to *as you ask the question*. If you think it is an open question, walk towards them. Besides the feeling of the energy of the speaker being taken away or brought towards the other person or people, this will also affect the person who has to answer, as they will have to use different vocal energy to reach the other character who is either at a distance from them or close.

Repeat the scene again without moving toward or away but in the memory of it.

Exercise 11

Open and closed questions are often used by barristers in court. It is a way of directing the interrogation of witnesses in favour of your argument.

Why not ask your actors to try an improvised conversation with open and closed questions? Perhaps you could set up a trial with defendants, prosecutors and witnesses. Could you make a trial using the characters and situation of the play you are working on?

Summary

- Exploring the use of open and closed questions within dialogue and debate can reveal insights into a character's nature.
- It can also clarify who is driving a scene and how they are doing so.

- Closed questions can be used in an attempt to quickly take control of a situation.
- Open questions can lead the debate more stealthily and subtly.

Here are some other texts where you could explore open and closed questions with these exercises:

David Hare, *The Absence of War*, Act 2, Scene 3.

Peter Hall's adaptation of George Orwell's *Animal Farm*, the end of Act 1. Explore the difference between Boxer's questions and Squealer's.

Githa Sowerby, *Rutherford and Son*, the scene in Act 2 between Rutherford and his daughter Janet. This scene can be explored through open and closed questions, vocabulary-appropriation exercises and listening exercises.

Status in Dialogue

Despite his apparent confidence, Birling reveals himself to be on the defensive, from the very beginning. His boastful confidence is an attempt to make **Ethos** work for him as he tries to persuade the Inspector that because of his business achievements and consequential standing within the community, he couldn't possibly be involved with the life of an ordinary working woman. The Inspector brings the status of his job with him into the room and doesn't appear to need to press his position. The scene is an example of how the authenticity of one character might be used to undermine that of another and how that is played out through the language they use.

Let's explore status.

Exercise 12

Using a piece of dialogue, establish the relative status of the characters. Ask the higher-status character to begin reading, walking about the space. The lower-status character should follow behind them and the dialogue should continue. If the lower-status character dislocates the conversation in any way they have to step in front (or turn around) and change leadership. This can happen as many times as the text dictates.

Status can be challenged and the flow of a conversation dislocated in different ways: by ignoring a question; answering a question with another question; changing the subject; or the strategic use of open and closed questions.

Repeat the dialogue without the actions but with the memory of the switching, or attempts at switching, status.

Exercise 13

This time, either one of the characters should lead the other around the space without deciding which is of the higher status. Whenever the character behind feels that they have the upper hand, they should step in front (or turn around) and the leadership will change.

This would be an interesting exercise to use on this section of *An Inspector Calls*, as both characters feel they are in charge.

Exercise 14

Place a chair in the middle of the room. This time the actors have to sit on the chair whenever they gain the advantage of the dialogue, giving way to the other if they gain the advantage.

If the surroundings are safe enough and the text suggests it, one actor could actively push the other off the chair. Or to enable the actor to feel their status strongly, they could stand on the chair when they gain ground.

Repeat the scene without the chairs. Can you retain the detail of the way the characters use language to try to gain or maintain status?

Summary

- It is always useful to recognise how status works within the specific world of your play, and if characters are aware of their own or others'.
- How does your character react to their status in relationship with others in the play?
- Can you see if they use rhetoric to work within the status they are given or to push against it?
- Seeing clearly how characters converse, how they respond to each other in dialogue, can reveal a lot about their personalities and the drive of their journey through the play.

Other texts where you could explore status with these exercises:

Tom Stoppard, *Rosencrantz and Guildenstern Are Dead*: any of the dialogue between the two main characters.

Shakespeare, *Much Ado About Nothing*, Act 1, Scene 1, the first exchange between Beatrice and Benedick.

Anton Chekhov, *Three Sisters*. You could explore Natasha's changing relationship with the family members in this way.

Samuel Beckett, *Waiting for Godot*. It is interesting to explore the relationship between Vladimir and Estragon through these exercises.

Harold Pinter, *The Birthday Party*, Act 2, Stanley and McCann.

Listening

Listening well is a vital skill for an actor. We often think we hear but do we really listen? A note I often give actors during previews and sometimes on press night is to raise their active listening. It can take some nerve, early on in the play's production, to really listen, as that is a time when you are understandably thinking more about your own lines and moves than about the other characters'. During previews, when you are still essentially rehearsing the play, you have many things to think about: changes from the director, changes to moves or costume and, if it is a new play, changes to lines. All these can stop you from listening properly, and then communication is not as authentic as it could be. But if you can hold your nerve and listen well, you usually find you can remember your own lines and thoughts better. Listening like this can then also help to deal with stage fright as your breath is regulated in response to your thoughts. Clearly hearing what other actors say helps your thought processes and responses.

Listening is also a very important issue for anyone involved in persuasion. You can't score points, win an argument or persuade somebody of something if you are not listening accurately to your opponent's point of view.

The characters we've looked at in *A Doll's House* and *Edward II* were listening to each other well, but Willy Loman in *Death of a Salesman* wasn't, and so was unable to move the debate forward. Listening was also an integral part of the conflict in the scene from *A Raisin in the Sun*.

Exercise 15

Reading the dialogue from any of our scenes again, or choosing another text, each speaker should repeat the last word or two, or phrase, that their opponent has spoken, before they speak their own lines.

If we look at the section from *A Doll's House*, we can see how it works.

MRS LINDE. I've learned to look at things practically. Life and poverty have taught me that.

KROGSTAD. **have taught me that**
And life has taught me to distrust fine words.

MRS LINDE. **taught me to distrust fine words**
Then it has taught you a useful lesson. But surely you still believe in actions?

KROGSTAD. **you still believe in actions**
What do you mean?

MRS LINDE. **what do you mean?**
You said you were like a shipwrecked man clinging to a spar.

KROGSTAD. **a shipwrecked man clinging to a spar**
I have good reason to say it.

MRS LINDE. **good reason to say it**
I'm in the same position as you. No one to care about, no one to care for.

KROGSTAD. **no one to care for**
You made your own choice.

MRS LINDE. **choice**
I had no choice – then.

KROGSTAD. **then**
Well?

MRS LINDE. **Well?**
Nils, suppose we two shipwrecked souls could join hands?

KROGSTAD. **join hands**
What are you saying?

MRS LINDE. **What are you saying?**
Castaways have a better chance of survival together than on their own.

When you have finished, speak the dialogue again without the repetition.

Exercise 16

Read the dialogue again but this time, instead of repeating the end of the other character's line, each speaker should repeat aloud the phrase or word they are responding to in their opponent's speech, before they speak their own. That could be from anywhere within the speech.

You will see that in the excerpt from *A Doll's House*, the words the characters are responding to are actually at the end of the other person's line. That isn't always the case. Try one of the other scenes I've explored or another you'd like to work on. You might find that the word or phrase they are responding to could even be in an earlier speech.

Then speak the dialogue again without the repetition.

Exercise 17

Another way to really listen to each other and to use words effectively is to speak the dialogue very quietly, as if you may be overheard. This leads to the need to be clear and precise.

Then repeat with normal voice.

These exercises are also very good for overcoming any tendency to drop the energy at the end of speeches. It's not only in Shakespeare that the most important word is often at the end of the line.

Listening exercises are useful for all dialogue scenes. They are often the first exercises I use with actors.

Summary

- Good listening is a vital skill for an actor. Remind yourself to turn up your listening when rehearsing and playing.
- Listening is also a vital skill for achieving success in a debate or argument.

- It is always interesting to see which characters are good listeners and which are not, and to think about why.

Listening exercises are useful whatever play you are working on. They are particularly good when you have learnt your lines. Then you really have to listen!

4.

Rhetorical
Patterns

LISTENING IS A VERY
IMPORTANT ISSUE FOR ANYONE
INVOLVED IN PERSUASION.

Three-part Structure: Storytelling

In my earlier look at speeches in plays, I concentrated on the three main Aristotelian persuasive strategies. I would now like to draw your attention to how the structure of a speech can be an important rhetorical element.

The point about rhetoric is that it is designed to be used in spoken argument. It is about making sure you are clearly heard, understood and believed. We could see it as part of the oral tradition which begins with storytelling. Rhetoric carries forward many of the devices that storytellers have used to engage the ear and the imagination of their listeners.

In any fairy story or folk tale that is well told, you will be familiar with the idea that it begins with a version of 'Once upon a time...' and ends with some sort of 'They all lived happily ever after'. In the middle is the story, of course. It is a classic storytelling technique that introduces a theme, characters and setting, then tells you what extraordinary events occurred in their lives, and finally tells you of the outcome or moral of the story.

Within the main story you will find new events, characters or themes that are introduced, explored or developed before a conclusion of some kind is reached about them. This simple structure of three parts is used to help the listener or reader to follow the progress of the story easily.

- Introduction
- Main story, including further events to be introduced, explored and concluded
- Conclusion

It's also the basic structure recommended for an essay or a thesis because it does the job. It draws the mind into a subject, then discusses or explores it, and eventually moves the ideas forward into some sort of change or development.

It's like a road map for a journey, or as if you, the reader as traveller, were taken by the hand and shown the path, the stepping stones. Or in rhetorical terms, it is the way a speaker leads the ear and the imagination of the listener in the direction they want them to go.

You will find that many speeches in plays can be divided into the same three parts: **Introduction**, **Exploration** and **Conclusion**.

Let's look at some examples.

In Act 3, Scene 3 of *Hamlet*, King Claudius wishes to atone for murdering his brother, Hamlet's father, and he is discovered trying to pray.

The structure I see in this speech is as follows:

Introduction

> O, my offence is rank, it smells to heaven;
> It hath the primal eldest curse upon't –
> A brother's murder.

Exploration

>   Pray can I not,
> Though inclination be as sharp as will,
> My stronger guilt defeats my strong intent,
> And, like a man to double business bound,
> I stand in pause where I shall first begin,
> And both neglect. What if this cursèd hand
> Were thicker than itself with brother's blood,
> Is there not rain enough in the sweet heavens

To wash it white as snow? Whereto serves mercy
But to confront the visage of offence?
And what's in prayer but this twofold force,
To be forestallèd ere we come to fall,
Or pardoned being down? Then I'll look up:
My fault is past. But, O, what form of prayer
Can serve my turn? 'Forgive me my foul murder'?
That cannot be, since I am still possessed
Of those effects for which I did the murder –
My crown, mine own ambition, and my queen.
May one be pardoned and retain th'offence?
In the corrupted currents of this world
Offence's gilded hand may shove by justice,
And oft 'tis seen the wicked prize itself
Buys out the law. But 'tis not so above:
There is no shuffling, there the action lies
In his true nature, and we ourselves compelled
Even to the teeth and forehead of our faults
To give in evidence. What then? What rests?
Try what repentance can. What can it not?
Yet what can it, when one cannot repent?
O wretched state! O bosom black as death!
O limèd soul, that struggling to be free
Art more engaged!

Conclusion

Help, angels! Make assay.
Bow, stubborn knees; and heart with strings of steel,
Be soft as sinews of the new-born babe.
All may be well.

The way to test this theory is to speak the **introduction** followed by the **conclusion**, missing out the **exploration** between them. They should make sense together. As these do.

O, my offence is rank, it smells to heaven;
It hath the primal eldest curse upon't –
A brother's murder.

...

Help, angels! Make assay.
Bow, stubborn knees; and heart with strings of steel,
Be soft as sinews of the new-born babe.
All may be well.

Beside this overall three-part structure, I see another within the **exploration**. That is the structure of the discussion of what Claudius should do to alleviate his feelings of guilt. This is how I see that structure.

He **introduces** his desire to pray.

Pray can I not,
Though inclination be as sharp as will,
My stronger guilt defeats my strong intent,
And, like a man to double business bound,
I stand in pause where I shall first begin,
And both neglect.

He then **explores** that. He looks at several elements, beginning with the bounty of heaven's 'forgiveness' and the impact of mercy and prayer, then 'What form of prayer' to use, followed by a question of being 'pardoned' and finally the possibility of 'repentance'.

What if this cursèd hand
Were thicker than itself with brother's blood,
Is there not rain enough in the sweet heavens
To wash it white as snow? Whereto serves mercy
But to confront the visage of offence?
And what's in prayer but this twofold force,

To be forestallèd ere we come to fall,
Or pardoned being down? Then I'll look up:
My fault is past. But, O, what form of prayer
Can serve my turn? 'Forgive me my foul murder'?
That cannot be, since I am still possessed
Of those effects for which I did the murder –
My crown, mine own ambition, and my queen.
May one be pardoned and retain th'offence?
In the corrupted currents of this world
Offence's gilded hand may shove by justice,
And oft 'tis seen the wicked prize itself
Buys out the law. But 'tis not so above:
There is no shuffling, there the action lies
In his true nature, and we ourselves compelled
Even to the teeth and forehead of our faults
To give in evidence. What then? What rests?
Try what repentance can. What can it not?
Yet what can it, when one cannot repent?

And he **concludes**:

O wretched state! O bosom black as death!
O limèd soul, that struggling to be free
Art more engaged!

So again, to test the choices made, read the **introduction** followed by the **conclusion**:

Pray can I not,
Though inclination be as sharp as will,
My stronger guilt defeats my strong intent,
And, like a man to double business bound,
I stand in pause where I shall first begin,
And both neglect.

...

O wretched state! O bosom black as death!
O limèd soul, that struggling to be free
Art more engaged!

We also find the same three-part structure in the work of more modern playwrights. Here is Gwendolen, sharing her opinion of men's names in Act 1 of Oscar Wilde's *The Importance of Being Earnest*:

Jack?… No, there is very little music in the name
Jack, if any at all, indeed. It does not thrill. It produces
absolutely no vibrations… I have known several
Jacks, and they all, without exception, were more
than usually plain. Besides, Jack is a notorious
domesticity for John! And I pity any woman who is
married to a man called John. She would probably
never be allowed to know the entrancing pleasure of a
single moment's solitude. The only really safe name is
Ernest.

Here's how it works. In the first place she is in a conversation with Jack, who she thinks is called Ernest, and she grabs the argument. He has said,

I think **Jack**, for instance, a charming name.

She picks up the name and throws it back at him:

Jack?… No, there is very little music in the name
Jack, if any at all, indeed. It does not thrill. It produces
absolutely no vibrations…

She then develops her theme –

I have known several **Jacks**, and they all, without
exception, were more than usually plain. Besides,
Jack is a notorious domesticity for **John**! And I pity
any woman who is married to a man called **John**. She

would probably never be allowed to know the entrancing pleasure of a single moment's solitude.

And confidently concludes her own debate with:

The only really safe name is **Ernest**.

Let's test it.

Jack?… No, there is very little music in the name Jack, if any at all, indeed. It does not thrill. It produces absolutely no vibrations…

…

The only really safe name is Ernest.

Here is Scene 4 of Tennessee Williams' *A Streetcar Named Desire*, in which Blanche expresses her opinion of her sister Stella's husband Stanley.

Let's unpick it. She introduces her theme:

He acts like an animal, has an animal's habits!

She explores it in detail:

Eats like one, moves like one, talks like one! There's even something – subhuman – something not quite to the stage of humanity yet! Yes, something – ape-like about him, like one of those pictures I've seen in anthropological studies! Thousands and thousands of years have passed him right by, and there he is – Stanley Kowalski – survivor of the Stone Age! Bearing the raw meat home from the kill in the jungle! And you – *you* here *waiting* for him! Maybe he'll strike you or maybe grunt and kiss you! That is, if kisses have been discovered yet! Night falls and the other apes gather! There in the front of the cave, all grunting like him, and swilling and gnawing and hulking! His poker night! – you call it – this party of apes! Somebody growls – some creature snatches at something – the fight is on! *God!* Maybe we are a long way from being made in God's image, but Stella – my sister – there has been *some* progress since then! Such things as art – as poetry and music – such kinds of new light have come into the world since then! In some kinds of people some tenderer feelings have had some little beginning! That we have got to make *grow*! And *cling* to, and hold as our flag!

She concludes:

In this dark march towards whatever it is we're approaching... *Don't – don't hang back with the brutes!*

Test it!

He acts like an animal, has an animal's habits!

...

In this dark march toward whatever it is we're approaching... *Don't – don't hang back with the brutes!*

However, you could see this passage in several sections. The first being her description of Stanley as 'an animal'. This begins, as does the whole passage, with:

He acts like an animal, has an animal's habits!

And concludes with:

Maybe he'll strike you or maybe grunt and kiss you! That is, if kisses have been discovered yet!

The next section is a continuation of her description of Stanley's animal-like behaviour, bringing in his friends. This has a separate three-part structure of its own and begins:

Night falls and the other apes gather!

Developing that idea with:

There in the front of the cave, all grunting like him, and swilling and gnawing and hulking! His poker night! – you call it – this party of apes!

And concludes with:

Somebody growls – some creature snatches at something – the fight is on! *God!*

Test it:

Night falls and the other apes gather!

…

Somebody growls – some creature snatches at something – the fight is on! *God!*

Then she considers the opposite of animal behaviour; her hope of man's higher aesthetic, which begins:

Maybe we are a long way from being made in God's image, but Stella – my sister – there has been *some* progress since then!

She then develops this argument:

Such things as art – as poetry and music – such kinds of new light have come into the world since then! In some kinds of people some tenderer feelings have had some little beginning!

And you could see this as concluding with:

That we have got to make *grow*! And *cling* to, and hold as our flag!

Let's test that:

Maybe we are a long way from being made in God's image, but Stella – my sister – there has been some progress since then!

...

That we have got to make *grow*! And *cling* to, and hold as our flag!

Looking for the repetition of this simple structure within long speeches is, I feel, a very important and effective way for an actor to be clear about and keep control of their argument.

This division of the text makes sure that you recognise and use the different persuasive elements of an argument or debate. It helps you to see how a character develops argument through their own experience, using specific ideas to paint pictures for the listener. It prevents the character's ideas being overwhelmed by one emotional drive and it opens out the argument for the listeners, both the other characters and audience.

Exercise 18

Use the texts above or any text that you think might fall into this structure.

Place three chairs apart in the room; one chair is for the **introduction**, one for the **exploration** and one for the **conclusion**. Go to the first chair, sit on it and speak aloud what you think might be the **introduction**. Then move to the second chair, sit on it and speak what you think might be the **exploration**. Finally move to the third chair, sit on it and speak the **conclusion**.

You might not find the divisions easily the first time you try. This is an exercise for experimentation. You can try different versions of the divisions.

Remember, the way to test this structure is to speak the **introduction** followed by the **conclusion**, missing out the **exploration**. If the beginning and the end make some sort of sense, you've probably found the structure.

If you don't have chairs you could simply move to three different parts of the room.

As always, repeat the text again without the moves but with the memory of them.

Summary

- Traditional storytelling is the foundation of many good plays.
- Introduction – Exploration – Conclusion is the basic structure of a good story.
- We find this structure in many speeches and if we trust it, our audience will follow our thoughts easily.
- Don't be afraid to dig deep into speeches to look for this structure: it really will help you unpick the detail of your character's thoughts.
- You will even find it in one single line of dialogue.

You will find the three-part structure in many texts, in both big speeches and in simple lines of dialogue. Here are some suggestions.

Tony Kushner, *Angels in America* – all the big speeches.

Conor McPherson, *The Weir* – the stories told by Finbar, Valerie, Jim and Jack.

David Hare: any of his plays.

George Farquhar, *The Beaux' Strategem* – the bigger speeches of Mrs Sullen, Dorinda, Aimwell and Archer.

Shakespeare – he uses it constantly. Look at any big speech, and you will find this format, but it can be seen in many shorter speeches too.

Tricolon or The Rule of Three

Groups of three seem to be very powerful. Going back to the oral tradition, many fairy stories tell of people being asked a question three times or doing a task three times. Usually, it is the third time or perhaps the third chance they have been given, that changes everything. I believe grouping ornaments, pictures or flower arrangements in threes is thought by interior designers to be aesthetically appealing. We hear it also in songs: 'Here, There and Everywhere'; 'Bewitched, Bothered and Bewildered'; 'In Dublin's fair city, where the girls are so pretty, I first set my eyes on sweet Molly Malone.'

In speech, there appears to be a rather satisfying and ear-catching rhythm to presenting ideas in three words, clauses or sentences. If you think about it, you may hear yourself using threes. It seems to be an instinctive way of presenting ideas that has a particular resonance to the ear and can therefore be used as a very powerful rhetorical device. (I've just done it here!)

In his book *Our Masters' Voices* (Routledge, 1984), Max Atkinson explored the use of threes in political rhetoric, recording in particular how the judicial use of groups of three in a speech leads directly to applause and presumably therefore to agreement or persuasion. This is known as a 'claptrap'.

'Veni, vidi, vici. I came, I saw, I conquered.' Julius
Caesar

'By your obedience to my general, by your concord in
the camp, and your valour in the field, we shall shortly
have a famous victory over these enemies of my God,
of my kingdom, and of my people.' Elizabeth I

'Government of the people, by the people, for the
people, shall not perish from the Earth.' Abraham
Lincoln

'Ask me my three main priorities for government, and I
tell you: Education, education, education.' Tony Blair

Playwrights use it too.

> HAMLET. O that this too too solid flesh would **melt**,
>   **Thaw** and **resolve** itself into a dew!
>
>   (*Hamlet*, Act 1, Scene 2)

> MACBETH. **Tomorrow** and **tomorrow** and **tomorrow**
>   Creeps in this petty pace from day to day
>   To the last syllable of recorded time
>
>   (*Macbeth*, Act 5, Scene 5)

> CHORUS. O for a Muse of fire that would ascend
>   The brightest heaven of invention,
>   **A kingdom for a stage, princes to act,**
>   **And monarchs to behold the swelling scene!**
>
>   (*Henry V*, Act 1, Scene 1)

Looking back at the plays we've already considered:

> OTHELLO. **Her father loved me, oft invited me,**
>   **Still questioned me the story of my life**
>   From year to year – **the battles, sieges, fortunes**
>   That I have passed.
>
>   (*Othello,* Act 1, Scene 3)

WALTER. The future, Mama. **Hanging over there at the edge of my days. Just waiting for me – a big, looming blank space** – full of *nothing*.
(A Raisin in the Sun)

WILLY. They laugh at me, heh? **Go to Filene's, go to the Hub, go to Slattery's, Boston.** Call out the name Willy Loman and see what happens! Big shot!
(Death of a Salesman)

And I could quote pages from the plays of David Hare, Patrick Marber and Tony Kushner, to name but three modern writers, who use it constantly. Have a look, try them out and see how useful it is to feel the rhythm and the specificity of this technique. Three elements have a cumulative feeling, building some sort of momentum in the journey of persuasion.

Exercise 19

If you find these groups of three in a text, it is useful to turn them into something tangible. Let's use those moveable objects again.

Using any three objects you have at hand – pencils, chairs, tables or people – as you speak each of the elements, physically take hold of the object and move them to another place. Or pile them up on top of each other.

If the person or people you are speaking to are present, give the object to them.

You could use three of the same object, but to be really specific, use three different objects or people.

Repeat the text again without the objects but with the memory of them.

Summary

- When a character uses a group of three, it enables them to land their point well, as threes seem to resonate with everyone.
- Don't be afraid to look for them and use them strategically.

You will find lists of three in almost any play you read. Look out for them.

Oppositions

Now, this is the big one! It seems to me that most plays are built around opposing elements. The central conflict, debate or drama is, as often as not, one state, desire or faction set off against another. Think of any of the great plays and playwrights you know: the Mystery Plays – Heaven v. Hell; Jacobean revenge tragedies – good v. evil; Chekhov – the past v. the future, age v. youth; David Hare – the Left v. the Right; Tennessee Williams, Arthur Miller, August Wilson – dreams v. reality. I could go on.

Then there is, of course, Shakespeare. It is one of the key elements to look for in his writing. He uses opposing ideas to make particular points, but an opposition can also be an integral part of a whole speech, scene or play, forming the structure that supports the hypothesis being played out. When an actor discovers this, it can often lead them and their audience to the heart of an argument. Through debate and contrast he reveals stories, characters' intentions, and the underlying themes of his plays.

The most commonly recognised type of opposition is **antithesis,** which is useful in drawing the ear of the listener, as its purpose is to bring us to the point being made by setting up an opposite first.

I'd like to share with you some work I did on *All's Well That Ends Well* when it was rehearsing for the Olivier Theatre. In case you don't know the play, here is the context for the speech, from Act 3, Scene 2, I would like to focus on.

When Helena's physician father died, she became the ward of the Countess of Roussillon. Helena is in love with the Countess's son Bertram, but he despises her for her low birth. Using the skills she learned from her father, she saves the life of the King of France, who then asks her what she would like as a reward. She says she wishes to marry Bertram and the King confirms the match. Bertram, however, spurns her, and leaves to fight in a war. When she is left alone she responds with this soliloquy, beginning with her quoting the letter Bertram has left her:

> HELENA. 'Till I have no wife, I have nothing in France.'
>   Nothing in France, until he has no wife!
>   Thou shalt have none, Roussillon, none in France;
>   Then hast thou all again. Poor lord! is't I
>   That chase thee from thy country and expose
>   Those tender limbs of thine to the event
>   Of the none-sparing war? and is it I
>   That drive thee from the sportive court, where thou
>   Wast shot at with fair eyes, to be the mark
>   Of smoky muskets? O you leaden messengers,
>   That ride upon the violent speed of fire,
>   Fly with false aim; move the still-peering air,
>   That sings with piercing; do not touch my lord.
>   Whoever shoots at him, I set him there;

Whoever charges on his forward breast,
I am the caitiff that do hold him to't;
And, though I kill him not, I am the cause
His death was so effected: better 'twere
I met the ravin lion when he roared
With sharp constraint of hunger; better 'twere
That all the miseries which nature owes
Were mine at once. No, come thou home, Roussillon,
Whence honour but of danger wins a scar,
As oft it loses all: I will be gone;
My being here it is that holds thee hence:
Shall I stay here to do't? No, no, although
The air of paradise did fan the house
And angels officed all: I will be gone,
That pitiful rumour may report my flight,
To consolate thine ear. Come, night; end, day!
For with the dark, poor thief, I'll steal away.

Exercise 20

This is an exercise I did with Michelle Terry, who was playing Helena.

I placed two rows of chairs at either side of the room; one row was Helena and the other Bertram, Count Roussillon.

I asked Michelle to begin the speech, standing at the top of the two rows of chairs. I then asked her, whenever she spoke about either of them, to sit on a chair in their rows, starting at those closest to her. If she made several consecutive points about either of them she should change chair within the same row. By doing this she was paying close attention to every detail of her argument.

She found herself going back sometimes but the aim was to see how the speech led her to a decision. It may work out differently for you, but the decision is made by comparing how many chairs you've sat on, on each side. You will see which way the argument is balanced.

This is one way in which the debate contained in the speech is structured.

To reveal another layer to the working out of this speech, try the following exercise.

Exercise 21

This time set up three chairs at a little distance from each other. One chair represents France/home, one represents war, and the third represents an outcast place, neither home nor war.

Speak the speech, sitting on the representative chairs as you speak of each of these elements.

Both these exercises are valid in helping the actor to work out the argument and to deliver it clearly.

As always, repeat the speech again without the exercise and try to carry forward what it taught you about the situation or character.

In *Antony and Cleopatra* there is an opposition at the heart of the play: Egypt v. Rome. Antony's dilemma is to reconcile his love of Cleopatra, Queen of Egypt, with his loyalty to Rome, which he has served as an heroic soldier for most of his life. This dilemma is played out in many different ways and in most scenes. Sometimes directly, as when he is challenged by Caesar, with whom he shares power in the Roman world. Sometimes indirectly, such as in the scene where he decides to fight the battle against Pompey by sea, a choice favoured by Cleopatra.

The style is set at the very beginning of the play:

> *Alexandria. A room in* CLEOPATRA*'s palace. Enter* DEMETRIUS *and* PHILO.

> PHILO. Nay, but this dotage of our general's
>   O'erflows the measure. Those his goodly eyes,
>   That o'er the files and musters of the war
>   Have glowed like plated Mars, now bend, now turn
>   The office and devotion of their view
>   Upon a tawny front. His captain's heart,
>   Which in the scuffles of great fights hath burst
>   The buckles on his breast, reneges all temper,
>   And is become the bellows and the fan
>   To cool a gipsy's lust. – Look where they come:
>   Take but good note, and you shall see in him
>   The triple pillar of the world transformed
>   Into a strumpet's fool. Behold and see.

I would ask the actor cast as Philo to play the oppositions strongly in order to establish the central theme and debate clearly for the audience. The issues set up here are repeated throughout the play: Antony's eyes bending away from war to pleasure; his passions, which had formerly been focused on soldiership, now devoted to sexual gratification; and his stature as a world leader reduced to the plaything of a lascivious woman.

Whilst playing the oppositions strongly, the actor playing Philo must also play them *persuasively*. If he concentrates on persuading Demetrius of his knowledge, he will be clear in his speech and at least begin to persuade the audience that the play contains a debate worth listening to.

Antitheses and oppositions are also at the heart of John Webster's plays. They carry argument and often reveal the underlying force of a character's personality. Here too they can form the very structure of the play. This is the case in *The Duchess of Malfi*, where the goodness and sincerity of the Duchess is seen in contrast to the malignant hypocrisy of her brothers and the court they have created. The thematic antithesis in this play is also established from the very first scene. It is then played out through opposing types of leadership, of love, fraternity and loyalty, and in the contrasts between honesty and hypocrisy, openness and secrecy.

The play opens with Antonio, the Duchess's steward, being welcomed home to Florence by his friend Delio. He has been in France and describes a well-governed court with 'their judicious king'; a court which has been purged of corrupt influences. He describes the king's rule there as inclusive, using a central metaphor of 'a common fountain, whence should flow / Pure silver-drops in general'.

In contrast, Bosola, the malcontent servant, describes the Cardinal and his brother Ferdinand (the Duchess's twin) as ruling this Italian court as 'like plum trees, that grow crooked over standing pools: they are rich, and o'erladen with fruit, but none but crows, pies and caterpillars feed on them'. Their court has 'flattering panders', and 'places in the court are but like beds in the hospital, where this man's head lies at that man's foot, and so lower and lower'.

I could choose many scenes to show you specific examples of antithesis. Here is Act 2, Scene 4. The Cardinal is Ferdinand and the Duchess's elder brother; Julia is his mistress.

Enter CARDINAL *and* JULIA.

CARDINAL. Sit: thou art my best of wishes. Prithee,
                                                    tell me
  What trick didst thou invent to come to Rome
  Without thy husband?

JULIA.   Why, my lord, I told him
  I came to visit an old anchorite
  Here, for devotion.

CARDINAL.   Thou art a witty false one!
  – I mean, to him.

JULIA.   You have prevailed with me
  Beyond my strongest thoughts. I would not now
  Find you inconstant.

CARDINAL.   Do not put thyself
  To such a voluntary torture, which proceeds
  Out of your own guilt.

JULIA.   How, my lord?

CARDINAL.   You fear
  My constancy because you have approved
  Those giddy and wild turnings in yourself.

JULIA. Did you e'er find them?

CARDINAL.   Sooth, generally for
                                                    women!
  A man might strive to make glass malleable
  Ere he should make them fixed.

JULIA.   So, my lord.

CARDINAL. We had need go borrow that fantastic
                                                    glass

Invented by Galileo the Florentine
To view another spacious world i' th' moon,
And look to find a constant woman there.

Constancy is the main subject of the debate here. Julia begins it:

You have prevailed with me
Beyond my strongest thoughts. I would not now
Find you **inconstant**.

The Cardinal takes up this word a couple of speeches later, and turns it to his own advantage, making her constancy the issue. He places it in antithesis to his own constancy:

You fear
My constancy because you have approved
Those **giddy and wild turnings in yourself**.

And then develops it:

CARDINAL.   Sooth, generally for women!
A man might strive to **make glass malleable**
Ere he should **make them fixed**.

JULIA.   So, my lord.

CARDINAL. We had need go borrow that fantastic
glass
Invented by Galileo the Florentine
To view **another spacious world i' th' moon**,
And look to find **a constant woman there**.

While here he is saying we need to look to another world to find a faithful woman, the moon is a well-known metaphor for changeability. He is therefore using an antithesis between 'th' moon' and 'constant' to add irony to his argument by hinting that even in the moon we wouldn't find a constant woman.

As the Cardinal uses antithesis to strengthen his argument, he also reveals his own suspicious nature.

JULIA. This is very well, my lord!

CARDINAL.   Why do you weep?
　Are tears your justification? The self-same tears
　Will fall into **your husband's bosom**, lady,
　With a loud protestation that you love **him**
　Above the world. Come, **I'll** love you wisely –
　That's jealously – since I am very certain
　You cannot make **me** cuckold.

In this exchange, I would point out to the actor that the comparisons continue, now between Julia's husband and 'I', the Cardinal. Actors are often wary of stressing personal pronouns, but sometimes they are where the argument lies.

JULIA.   I'll go home
　To my husband.

CARDINAL.   You may thank me, lady.
　I have taken you off your melancholy perch,
　Bore you upon my fist, and show'd you game,
　And let you fly at it. – I pray thee, kiss me. –
　When thou wast with thy husband, thou wast
　　　　　　　　　　　　　　　　watched
　Like a tame elephant. – Still you are to thank me. –
　Thou hadst only kisses from him and high feeding;
　But what delight was that? 'Twas just like one
　That hath a little fingering on the lute,
　Yet cannot tune it. – Still you are to thank me.

Here the Cardinal uses the opposition between two animals to illustrate how he sees Julia's current position. Yet both of them are animals controlled by men: a bird of prey, he has taken

> **off your melancholy perch,**
> **Bore you upon my fist, and showed you game,**
> **And let you fly at it**

compared to how with her husband,

> **thou wast watched**
> **Like a tame elephant**

and

> **Thou hadst only kisses from him and high feeding**

Here are some exercises to help you feel how the oppositions play out.

Exercise 22

Holding the text in one hand, change hands when you come to the first part of an antithesis or opposition, changing again on the opposite.

Repeat without changing hands.

Exercise 23

Set up two chairs and stand in between them. Move to one and sit on it to speak the first part of the antithesis and then to the other for the second part. Don't rush this; move between the seats without speaking, then speak when you sit. This will clarify the exact language used. You could call one seat positive and the other negative.

Repeat without using the chairs.

Summary

- Oppositions are used to lay out or clarify a point of view.
- Look for them in your character's speeches and play them strongly.
- They can be powerful elements in persuasion and in storytelling.
- You will also find it useful to identify an opposition that is central to the drama as a whole.

Other texts where you could explore oppositions with these exercises:

Timberlake Wertenbaker, *Our Country's Good*, Act 1, Scene 8 ('The Women Learn Their Lines').

R. C. Sherriff, *Journey's End*. Characters in this play constantly use antitheses to tell their stories.

George Etherege, *The Man of Mode*. The young rakes and men about town, Dorimant, Medley and Young Bellair, use antithesis as part of their wit.

Terence Rattigan, *After the Dance*. David is especially fond of presenting his argument through the use of oppositions but you will find many of the other characters use them from time to time also.

George Farquhar, *The Beaux' Strategem*. Mrs Sullen frequently uses witty antitheses to support her point of view.

Ben Jonson, *Volpone* and other of his plays. Characters who feel they have the upper hand tend to present their cleverness through the use of antithesis.

5.

Wordplay, Imagery and Figurative Language

METAPHOR AND SIMILE ARE
POWERFUL TOOLS IN THE
RHETORIC WORKBOX.

Metaphor and Simile

Earlier on in this book I talked about how listening to your opponent's argument is vital if you want to gain ground in some way. You must also, of course, be sure to draw their ear to your own argument.

A powerful way to do this is to stimulate the listener's imagination through the use of imagery in **metaphor** and **simile**. The English language is full of metaphor and simile: hard as nails, paper thin, dead drunk, someone who is a pain in the neck or putty in your hands; it's endless.

Metaphor is a way of enhancing meaning by placing upon a word or idea, the characteristics of something else.

Poets use figures of speech and so do playwrights. As in these quotations from *Othello*:

> The very head and front of my offending
> Hath this extent, no more.

> She'd come again, and with a greedy ear
> Devour up my discourse

> O, beware, my lord, of jealousy!
> It is the green-eyed monster, which doth mock
> The meat it feeds on.

If it is an extended metaphor (like the shipwreck we noticed earlier in the excerpt from *A Doll's House*), it can create not just a picture in the mind of the listener but a narrative.

Simile is a type of metaphor and is a more direct comparison of one thing with another. You know it is a simile because the words 'like' or 'as' will be used in the comparison.

As right as rain, like candy from a baby

We heard Claudius in *Hamlet* praying that his

>   heart with strings of steel,
>   Be soft as sinews of the new-born babe.

In *The Duchess of Malfi*, simile is another very significant element of Webster's rhetoric. The text is very rich with them; it seems to be the way in which characters most like to explain themselves. It extends Webster's device of contrast and comparison through which he wishes us to consider the use of power in this world.

Plays of the Jacobean period deal with passionate responses to corruption in society. It is very easy for actors to be drawn deeply into the passion at the expense of the argument. So, as you explore and enjoy the use of simile in *The Duchess of Malfi*, be sure to use them to persuade the person you are speaking to of your point of view, or maybe of your feelings.

You could take any section from the play and find plenty of simile, here are some:

Ferdinand to Bosola:

>   This will gain
>   Access to private lodgings, where yourself
>   May, **like a politic dormouse**...
>   (Act 1, Scene 2)

Ferdinand to the Cardinal, his brother:

>   Think't the best voyage
>   That e'er you made; **like the irregular crab,**
>   Which, though't goes backward, thinks that it goes
>   right
>   Because it goes its own way.
>   (Act 1, Scene 3)

Antonio to the Duchess:

> And may our sweet affections, **like the spheres,**
> **Be still in motion!**
>
> (Act 1, Scene 3)

The Cardinal to Julia, his mistress:

> When thou wast with thy husband, thou wast watch'd
> **Like a tame elephant.** – Still you are to thank me. –
> Thou hadst only kisses from him and high feeding;
> But what delight was that? **'Twas just like one**
> **That hath a little fingering on the lute.**
>
> (Act 2, Scene 4)

The use of imagery is a heightened form of expression and so associated with poetry. It is not surprising therefore, that in Shakespeare it is often found when lovers speak. To find examples to work with, I suggest you look at any of the lovers' scenes in *A Midsummer Night's Dream*, starting from Act 1, Scene 1; and *Romeo and Juliet*, Act 1, Scene 5, when Romeo first sees Juliet, or Act 3, Scene 2, when he sees her at her window. These young people are presented as in love with love and seem to be delighted to be using the traditional language of love.

> LYSANDER. How now, my love! Why is your cheek so
> pale?
> How chance the roses there do fade so fast?

> HERMIA. Belike for want of rain, which I could well
> Beteem them from the tempest of mine eyes.
> (*A Midsummer Night's Dream*, Act 1, Scene 1)

> DEMETRIUS. O, how ripe in show
> Thy lips, those kissing cherries, tempting grow;
> This pure congealèd white, high Taurus' snow,

Fanned with the eastern wind, turns to a crow
When thou hold'st up thy hand. O, let me kiss
That princess of pure white, this seal of bliss!
>> (*A Midsummer Night's Dream*, Act 3, Scene 2)

ROMEO. But, soft! What light through yonder window
>> breaks?
It is the east, and Juliet is the sun!
Arise, fair sun and kill the envious moon,
Who is already sick and pale with grief,
That thou her maid art far more fair than she.
>> (*Romeo and Juliet*, Act 2, Scene 2)

In this speech, beside the **analogy** of Juliet being the sun, there is also the **personification** of the moon. **Analogy** is the comparison on one thing with another. **Personification** is to give human characteristics to something that isn't human. Both are also forms of metaphor and intended to add clarity to meaning by creating vivid or perhaps unexpected pictures in the imagination of the listener.

Expressing Feelings Actively

For me it is essential that actors see the use of imagery and comparison as a means of communication. I always encourage them to be sure their focus is on getting into the mind of the person they are speaking to rather than solely expressing how they feel. There is a danger that they can fall in love with the experience of their own feelings. As I have already mentioned, it was Aristotle who spoke of the need for arguments to be 'found' and he also said that it takes art to do so. This seems to me to be the essence of the actor's craft.

Most actors will begin the exploration of their character by looking for emotional truth. It is a fundamental element of modern, realistic acting techniques, and this truthful, authentic representation of a character is what actors, directors and voice coaches today want and what audiences expect. However, once this work begins to feel right for the actor, they should then speak the text as a means of furthering their character's needs and journey within the play, and not just to express how they feel at any given moment.

My experience is that when actors focus only on showing how their characters feel, the text easily becomes unclear. The audience will probably know they are feeling something strongly but the feeling will appear generalised; unspecific. My advice is always to speak *from* the character's feelings not *to* them. The text needs to be used actively and persuasively, in a way that engages with the action of the moment, the scene or the whole play, for us to understand the whys and wherefores of the drama. When I was working at the Royal Shakespeare Company, Cicely Berry told me she felt that audiences are more interested in the character's thoughts than their feelings. I agree with her and suggest we need to treat reflection and the internalisation of feelings with care. This can be when the audience will fail to hear the story properly and get lost.

Exercise 24

This exercise is to clarify the balance and persuasive power of similes.

Use a small ball or anything you can hold in the palm of your hand to throw and catch.

As you speak the element of the text that is being compared, that is the first part of the simile, pick up the ball in one of your hands, as if holding the image. If the image contains more than one element, throw the ball up on the relevant word or phrase and catch. When you speak the comparison, toss or pass the ball to the other hand on the relevant word or phrase, again throwing up and catching if more than one.

So, using the example I gave of the section of dialogue between Julia and The Cardinal in Act 2, Scene 4 of *The Duchess of Malfi*, you would pick up the ball on 'watch'd', then change hands for 'a tame elephant'. Change hands again for 'delight'. Then change again for 'a little fingering on the lute'.

Repeat the exercise without the ball but with the memory of the details.

Exercise 25

This exercise helps you to make strong connections with the images used in metaphors and to share them.

Using a whiteboard or simply pieces of paper, draw the image you are using as you speak it; showing it to the listener as you do so. If there are lots of images you could use different pieces of paper or build them up on one big sheet or board.

When you have finished, speak the dialogue again without the drawings but with the memory of them.

You could use Exercise 6, the furniture exercise, for figures of speech, creating the image in sculpture.

Metaphor and simile are powerful tools in the rhetorical workbox. They can be used as **Pathos**, appealing to the emotions, or **Logos** when the comparison of one thing to another can be a way of presenting evidence to support your argument or idea. Aristotle said: 'Metaphor brings about learning.'

Summary

- We can consider figurative language – metaphor and simile – to be rhetorical devices.
- They appeal to the imagination of the listener and by doing so they can help to persuade them of your point of view.
- Look out for imagery in your character's dialogue so that you can use it as part of their persuasive tactics.
- Figurative language can also tell you more about your character if you explore the type of imagery they choose.

Other texts where you could explore figurative language with these exercises:

Thomas Middleton, *Women Beware Women*. Look for who uses natural imagery and who uses that of food and appetite. What does it say about them?

Ben Jonson, *Volpone*. Notice the animal, bird and fish imagery used. The exercises will help to reveal each character's nature through their choice of imagery.

Shakespeare, *Macbeth*. Use the exercises to illuminate images of light and dark, blood, water and birds.

Shakespeare's *Henry V* is rich in metaphor. The exercises will enable you to use them actively.

Alliteration and Assonance

The link between sound and sense in language was important in early rhetorical theories. Aristotle and other teachers of rhetoric were aware of how sound and rhythm could be used to get their argument into the ears of their listeners. So were the early storytellers. **Alliteration** and **assonance** are tools they frequently used. **Alliteration** is the use of repeated consonant sounds and **assonance** is repeated vowels. I recently heard a radio programme about early Welsh stories, which were full of alliteration.

The first plays in English were the religious Mystery or Miracle Plays and the secular 'Mummers' plays'. These can be viewed as an extension of the storytelling tradition. They were generally played outside by travelling players and the earliest texts of Mummers' plays to survive are from the eighteenth century. The Mystery Plays used alliteration very strongly to help their listeners to hear the plays and connect deeply with their spiritual message. It was a particular feature of all early and medieval English literature. You will find it in the Old English epic *Beowulf* and in Chaucer and other writers of the Middle English period. The Mystery Plays were played first in churches and then outside, so the alliteration would also have helped to send the words out.

Feel how meaning is enhanced by the alliteration in this section ('The Harrowing of Hell') from the York Mystery Plays.

Jesus manne on <u>molde</u>, be <u>meke</u> to me *earth, obedient*

And have thy Maker in thi mynde,
And thynke howe I have <u>tholid</u> for thee *suffered*
With <u>pereles</u> paynes for to be <u>pyned</u>. *unequalled, suffered*
The <u>forward</u> of my <u>Fadir</u> free *covenant, father*

Have I fulfillid, as folke may fynde;
Therfore aboute nowe woll I bee
That I have bought for to unbynde.
The <u>feende thame wanne with trayne</u>   *devil has won with*
                                                trickery

Thurgh <u>frewte</u> of erthely foode;   *fruit*
I have thame getyn agayne
Thurgh bying with my bloode.

You could pick any of the plays from the York, Towneley or Chester cycles of Mystery Plays; they are all full of alliteration. They are easily found online with notes on the words you might not know, or in modern spelling. However, I encourage you to try to speak them in their original form because it is so muscular and descriptive.

These are wonderful pieces to speak and terrific exercises for actors. Practising the exercises in this section on pieces of text high in the use of alliteration and assonance will help you to recognise when they occur in more modern pieces and will have prepared you to use them with dexterity. No one wants an actor to labour this type of language, it needs to be handled easily so that you can respond to it in the way that your character would.

Ben Jonson carries forward some of the alliterative taste of his predecessors. Here's a speech from Act 3 of *Sejanus*.

MACRO. I will not ask why Caesar **b**ids do this,
  But joy that he **b**ids me. It is the **b**liss
  Of courts to be e**m**ployed, not **m**atter how:
  A **p**rince's **p**ower makes all his actions virtue.
  We, whom he **w**orks by, are du**m**b instruments,
  To do, but not enquire: his great intents
  Are to be **s**erved, not **s**earched. Yet as that **b**ow

> Is **m**ost in hand whose owner **b**est doth know
> T'affect his ai**m**s, so let that states**m**an hope
> **M**ost use, **m**ost **p**rice, can hit his **p**rince's scope.

The alliteration throughout this speech is in consonants that are made with the lips: *b*, *p*, *m* and *w*. It is up to the individual actor or director to interpret this but maybe there is a sensuality here?

There are other rhetorical devices going on here too. There is the metaphor of the bowman letting loose his arrow –

> Yet as that bow
> Is most in hand whose owner best doth know
> T'affect his aims

– used as a comparison with the 'statesman' who needs to practise or pay to serve his prince.

Then there is the use of line-end rhymes. Rhyme is another strong way to get your message into the ear of the listener and I want to encourage you to make friends with it. Don't be afraid of allowing the rhymes to have their place and be heard. In the passage above, the rhymes of 'bow' and 'know', 'hope' and 'scope' occur at the end of lines, where the meaning runs on from one to the other. Don't feel you have to stop on the words 'bow' and 'hope' but if you land on them firmly and then keep the sense going, you will open up the meaning for the listeners.

In *A Midsummer Night's Dream*, Shakespeare famously uses rhyme relentlessly. It is there sometimes to help create the supernatural elements of the play, sometimes to emphasise the youthful romantic desires of the lovers. It always adds to the joy and comedy.

Of course, there are plenty of examples of **alliteration** and **assonance** in Shakespeare's plays, such as here, in Act 5, Scene 1 of *Macbeth*.

> LADY MACBETH. **Out**, damned spot! **Out** I say! One; two: why, then, 'tis **time** to do't. Hell is murky! **Fie**, my lord, **fie**! A soldier and **afeard**? What need we **fear** who knows it, when none can call **our power** to **account**? Yet who would have thought the old man to have had so **much blood** in him?

Notice the assonance in '**Out**... **out**', and '**our** p**ow**er to acc**ou**nt'; 't**i**me... F**ie**, my lord, f**ie**!' At the end, 'so m**u**ch bl**oo**d'. (Remember assonance is heard in the sound of the vowel and not always seen in its spelling.)

And there is also alliteration in '**F**ie... **f**ie... **a**feard... **f**ear'.

We hear it also in Act 3, Scene 3 of *Coriolanus*, where its hero cries:

> You **c**ommon **c**ry of **c**urs! Whose **b**reath I hate
> As **r**eek o'the **r**otten fens, whose loves I prize
> As the dead **c**ar**c**ases of un**b**uried men
> That do **c**orrupt my air, I **b**anish you.

Speak this and feel how powerfully those consonants can carry his feelings and intention!

Exercise 26

To feel how alliteration, the repeated use of consonants, works in your mouth, begin by gently whispering the text. Be careful that you are not pushing the air out through your throat and mouth. Let it be soft. Your aim is to feel where the tongue and lips are placed to make the different consonants and how to quickly and accurately move between them. You should also enjoy the feeling of the breath passing through the mouth at the point where these consonants are made. Repeat the whispered text several times.

(If you wish to know more about how consonants are made, see Chapter One in my book *The Voice Exercise Book*.)

Once you have whispered the text a few times, speak it quietly but clearly. Try to maintain your awareness of how each consonant is made. Repeat this several times.

Then speak the text at the right volume to be heard in the space you are to work in, whether it is a room, hall or stage. Again, repeat this several times.

Exercise 27

Once you feel confident with the articulation of your text, try speaking it, quite quietly but very fast. Repeat several times.

Then speak it again at the louder volume and normal speed.

Exercise 28

To enhance your connection with vowel sounds, for when you come across assonance, try the following sequence.

Begin by silently 'mouthing' the text. Don't overdo this but be sure to keep your jaw free so that your tongue and lips can move easily. Your aim is to become more aware of the particular shape of vowels in your mouth; how your tongue and lips move to make them. Repeat several times.

Then, as in the above exercise, speak the text quite quietly to feel the resonance within the vowel shapes in your mouth. Again, don't overexaggerate the shapes but be conscious of them. Repeat several times.

Finally, speak the text aloud with your heightened awareness of the shapes you are making.

Exercise 29

Also, to feel the movement of vowel shapes in your mouth, try 'intoning' your text. That is, speaking it on one note only, almost like a chant, but keeping it completely smooth, without any expressive movement in your voice.

In this exercise you should enjoy the feeling of your resonant voice flowing out of your mouth as it passes through the vowel and consonant sounds.

Then speak the text again normally but see if you can retain the feeling of the flow of sound as it moves through normal speech.

The power of assonance is because vowels carry emotion. Think of singing, which is a heightened expression of emotion. As we sing we sustain sound through lengthened vowels. Therefore, assonance can be used in **Pathos**, when we want to move our listeners' emotions.

Summary
- Wordplay, imagery and figurative language are all useful rhetorical tools.
- Metaphor and simile offer images with which you can surprise your listeners and stimulate their imagination.
- The repetitive nature of alliteration and assonance

can emphasise particular thoughts and make them memorable.

- Don't be afraid of them but don't overstress them. If you articulate them clearly, they speak for themselves.
- When you are expressing your character's feelings, be sure to keep the language active and persuasive. You need to be specific with your words for your thoughts and feeling to be clear.
- Take care that your emotions don't overwhelm your words.

Other texts where you could explore the use of alliteration and assonance with these exercises:

Timberlake Wertenbaker, *Our Country's Good*, Act 1, Scene 10 ('John Wisehammer and Mary Brenham Exchange Words').

Thomas Middleton, *Women Beware Women*. When passions rise, the characters find both alliteration and assonance powerful. For example, Act 3, Scene 2 (Leantio); Act 4, Scene1 (the Duke); Act 4, Scene 2 (Livia).

David Hare, *The Absence of War*. Look closely at George's speeches. His rhetoric often includes alliteration and assonance.

6.

Code
Language

CODE LANGUAGE CAN BE A VERY
POWERFUL RHETORICAL TOOL.

It can be surprising how much of the language we use every day could be considered 'code language'. Code language is any language or vocabulary that is specifically related to one group of people. That could be a group linked by work, country, ethnicity, religion, social group or even sport or hobby. For example, in theatre, we speak of 'upstage', 'downstage', 'stage-right', 'stage-left' and 'green room'; an actor might be 'upstaging', 'off-book' or 'dropping lines'. Today we talk of acting processes as 'method acting' or 'actioning'.

It is usual for each new generation to invent a code of language to baffle their elders or separate themselves from them. In the 1920s you could be 'goofy about a hoofer' (in love with a dancer) or have a 'crush on a spiffy sheik' (be infatuated with an elegant, sexy man). Today the language of popular music and modern media can confound the older generation: your 'squad' could be really 'live' but have to be 'woke' to stay 'lit' (your group of friends could be really cool or fun but have to be aware of current trends to stay amazing). Today trends move so fast that this slang may well be out of date before this book is published.

You could also consider that accent or dialect can be considered code language. Especially if it is introduced or used in a strong form amongst people who don't use it. Code language binds groups together and can exclude people not of the same group.

Within a play, any type of code language can be a very powerful rhetorical tool, especially when arguing from **Ethos**. Through the use of code language, a character can establish themself as being authentically part of a group or have knowledge of a group through use of its codes. Or they could exclude their opponent from a powerful group and in doing so move the argument in a direction they can easily control. They could also use code language to move the emotions of a listener or group of listeners (**Pathos**) by tapping into their language.

Let's go to Shakespeare again. Here is the first part of a speech made by Prince Hal in *Henry IV, Part 1*, Act 2, Scene 4, speaking to Poins, one of the frequenters of the Boar's Head Tavern in Eastcheap, London.

> PRINCE HAL. With three or four **loggerheads** amongst three of four score **hogsheads**. I have sounded the very bass-string of humility. Sirrah, I am sworn brother to a **leash of drawers**; and can call them all by their christen names, as Tom, Dick, and Francis. They take it already upon their salvation, that though I be but Prince of Wales, yet I am the king of courtesy; and tell me flatly I am no **proud Jack**, like Falstaff, but a **Corinthian**, a **lad of mettle**, a **good boy**, by the Lord, so they call me, and when I am King of England, I shall command **all the good lads** in Eastcheap. They call drinking deep, **dyeing scarlet**; and when you breathe in your watering, they cry **'hem!' and bid you play it off**. To conclude, I am so good a proficient in one quarter of an hour, that I can drink with **any tinker** in his own language during my life.

We have already met the prince in the company of his dissolute friend Sir John Falstaff in Act 1, Scene 2. We have heard him in lively and informal conversation with the knight. Now, in the company of the 'rude society' (as his father later calls his Eastcheap comrades), he boasts about his ability to slip easily into the code language of the East London tavern.

Compare this with his reply to his father in Act 3, Scene 2, when the King has questioned the company he has been keeping:

PRINCE HAL. So please your majesty, I would I could
    Quit all offences with as clear excuse
    As well as I am doubtless I can purge
    Myself of many I am charged withal:
    Yet such extenuation let me beg,
    As, in reproof of many tales devised,
    Which oft the ear of greatness needs must hear,
    By smiling pick-thanks and base news-mongers,
    I may, for some things true, wherein my youth
    Hath faulty wandered and irregular,
    Find pardon on my true submission.

The code language here is largely in the style of speech. First of all he speaks in verse which instantly implies formality. His syntax is educated and courtly and suggests he is speaking to people who can follow a complex argument. The sentence structure is convoluted and elaborate. He speaks in one long sentence, and through a couple of parentheses, takes a long time to get to his point.

In his speech to Poins, the code language is mainly in his vocabulary and in the direct, confident, firm verbs: 'I have... I am... I shall'. Whereas speaking to his father he is more indirect: 'I would I could... I am doubtless... I may'.

Henry is able to code-switch, to change the style of his speech and his vocabulary according to the occasion, or the group of people to whom he is talking. A very useful talent to have in the persuasion game.

In the play *Small Island*, adapted for the stage by Helen Edmundson from Andrea Levy's novel, code language is dotted throughout. It serves several functions in the play: it authentically defines and characterises different groups of people; it enhances the historical period of the action; and, on at least one occasion, it is used as a persuasive strategy.

In Act 1, Scene 3, we are in the RAF recruiting office in Kingston, Jamaica, in 1943. Gilbert is there to join up.

OFFICER 1 (*referring to a form in his hand*). So. Gilbert Joseph.

GILBERT. That's me.

OFFICER 1. Born in Jamaica. Both your parents British-Jamaican?

GILBERT. Yes, sir. Although my father is Jewish. Was Jewish. I don't know if that...

OFFICER 2. Good Lord! I didn't know there were any Jews in Jamaica.

GILBERT. Oh, yes, sir. There are quite a number of Jews here. But my father is a Christian now. Ever since he met Jesus on the **battlefield at Ypres**. He says the Lord shared a tin of fish with him and lent him some writing paper. He only says this when he's drunk, mind.

OFFICER 1. Well. Jewish heritage. Even more reason to join the fight against Herr Hitler.

GILBERT. Yes, sir.

OFFICER 1. You've passed some exams, I see.

GILBERT. Yes. At St John's College. It is my plan to go to a university and study the Law. I mean to be a lawyer.

OFFICER 2. Do you?

OFFICER 1. Excellent. Well, you're certainly the **sort of chap** we need. With these grades we'll be getting you trained up as **a wireless operator, an air gunner.** Perhaps **a flight engineer – second only to a pilot in terms of respect.** How does that sound?

GILBERT (*delighted and surprised*). That sounds fine, sir.

OFFICER 1. Then after the war, with **an impressive service record,** I think **Civvy Street** will positively welcome you for further study.

He stands. GILBERT *stands too.* OFFICER 1 *shakes* GILBERT's *hand.*

Congratulations. Good man.

In acting terms, it is very important that these words are spoken clearly. In a very short scene, they quickly create the specialised world of the 1940's RAF; a world, perhaps a club, that Gilbert is keen to join. A world that 'sounds fine' to him. However, I'm not suggesting these words and phrases should be exaggerated by the actor; they must be heard as natural vocabulary for the officers, although there is a sense that they are being used to excite Gilbert, and encourage him to join (**Pathos**).

This world and its codes are in striking contrast to the language used by Gilbert's cousin Elwood who appears immediately following this exchange. In a wonderful juxtaposition, Elwood brings with him the colloquial language of Jamaica at this time, and with it the political focus of their homeland. He says:

Why you wanna go **licky-licky** to the British?

And:

> **Cha**, this is **a white man's war**. Why you wanna
> **lose your life for a white man**?

And then:

> ELWOOD. **Lose your life for Jamaica.**
> **Independence** – that is worth a fight. Lose your life
> **to see a black man in the Governor's house doing**
> **more than just sweeping the floor**. This war will
> change nothing for you and me.

> GILBERT. It will get me **off this island** for one thing.
> And I will be an **air gunner**. And I will go to **an**
> **English university**.

> ELWOOD. Is that what they tell you? Man, **the**
> **English are liars**. They tell you anything **to make**
> **you do their dirty work**.

The argument is carried in the political code language of
Jamaica at this particular time and in Gilbert's reply. Elwood
uses it for both **Logos** ('These are the things that will
change') and **Pathos** ('You should feel angry at the way the
British treat us'). Gilbert won't be baited and sticks to **Logos**
('This is what signing up will achieve for me').

Working with the actors on this scene when it was produced
at the National Theatre, I also asked them to make the story
very clear by noting and playing the opposition between
'the British' and 'Jamaica'; between 'the white man' and 'a
black man'.

Code language of the war and the armed forces can be
heard in this play in both Jamaica and England. It is there
in Act 1, Scene 2 – set in a London rest centre for people
whose homes have been bombed; and in Act 1, Scene

4, when Hortense and Gilbert first meet at a Jamaican homecoming celebration, with Hortense asking him about her cousin Michael who is missing in action. Back in London it is heard again in Act 1, Scene 5, when Queenie goes to the War Office to enquire about her missing husband, Bernard.

The Empress by Tanika Gupta also depicts events when a country in the British Empire – this time India – is looking towards independence. The central story of the play is the relationship between the elderly Queen Victoria and Abdul Karim, one of her Indian servants. Around this story, several other stories of Indian people in England are told.

In this part of Act 2, Scene 5, Dadabhai Naoroji has just won a British Parliamentary seat. He is celebrating with his supporters and Sita, a young woman who came to England as an ayah, a nanny to a British family, who abandoned her at Tilbury Docks. She has since become Naoroji's secretary.

We are in a drawing room, Indian in décor. Dawn is rising and SITA *rushes in to light the lamps as a group of Indian and English* MEN *and* WOMEN *follow her in. They are in high spirits as they carry* DADABHAI NAOROJI *in.* SITA *looks startled at first but is pleased.*

WILLIAM. The **new Member of Parliament for the constituency of Finsbury**!

RAJA. **The British electorate** have finally kicked Salisbury in the guts and **elected a 'black man'**.

DADABHAI (*laughing*). For goodness' sake, put me down! I'm going to fall, you are all too intoxicated… Sita, do tell them to put me down.

The MEN *all carefully place* DADABHAI *on the ground.* SITA *helps him to a chair.*

What time is it?

SITA. It is five in the morning, Dada.

DADABHAI. I am quite overcome with the emotion of the night.

WILLIAM. So you should be. **Your constituents** were jubilant at your victory tonight.

RAJA. You could hear the cheering at St Paul's at one side and Chelsea Hospital on the other.

DADABHAI. I only just won – **very slim margin. A majority of five over the Tory candidate**. There is much work to be done.

WILLIAM. Our Dada is the **first Indian man to represent his country in Parliament**. The very first!

SITA *picks up a small bundle of papers.*

SITA. Telegrams have been arriving through the night, Dada.

She hands them over to DADABHAI *who looks through them.*

DADABHAI. 'Congratulations from Keir Hardie. See you in **the Commons**.' Excellent, **he won the seat for Westham South**... 'Finally we have you. John Bright...' 'The journey has just begun my friend. My congratulations Dada. Ramsay Macdonald.' 'Rejoice beyond measure that you have been **elected Liberal MP for Central Finsbury**.' Florence Nightingale.

WILLIAM. This is the advantage of supporting **women's suffrage** Dada. You have more lady supporters than any **MP** I know.

Everyone laughs. DADABHAI *continues to smile and peruse the telegrams.*

DADABHAI. Please, sit close to me, Sita. Raja, get Sita some cordial. You see? One month here and already I am completely dependent on this little girl.

WILLIAM. How did you manage without her before, Dada?

RAJA *gets busy pouring some drinks.* SITA *sits down.*

JOSEPHINE. Did you see the faces of your betrayers? They are an insult to the name of the **British Liberal Party**.

DADABHAI. There's no need to gloat, Josephine.

JOSEPHINE. I don't know how you can be so magnanimous when those snakes... to try and prevent you from **standing for election**... to have refused to back down, **claiming neutrality** when that fool Ford **stood for election** and almost risked **splitting the vote down the middle**.

WILLIAM. **The Liberal Party** should have given you the wholehearted backing you deserved. By not doing so, it leaves a bad taste in one's mouth.

DADABHAI. My friends, it is all in the past. We are victorious.

In this scene it is also essential that the actors speak the names of the people they are referring to very clearly. Their inclusion in the scene emphasises when in British history this significant event occurred.

Now, you may feel as you read these scenes, that the placement of this language is obvious. That may be so, but my experience when working alongside actors who are creating these roles is that the importance of this sort of language can sometimes be missed. They don't always recognise it as code and, as they focus on truthful characterisation, storytelling through such details of the text can be overlooked. That is when the outside ear of the voice coach or director is vital.

Exercise 30

Using any text that you feel includes code language, as you speak the text, tap yourself on the chest every time you use any code language from your group. Or you could tap the arm of the other characters in your group when you wish to include them or if they wish to be included in a group.

Repeat the text without the tapping but in the memory of it.

Exercise 31

As you speak the text, you could push away the people or person you wish to exclude as you speak code words or phrases.

Repeat the text without the pushing but in the memory of it.

Exercise 32

Speak the text again but this time draw your group to you as you speak your code words or phrases.

Repeat without the physical actions.

Recognising how codes are used within a play can help the actor or director to explore layers of relationship and transaction between characters. It is another way of looking for clues within the language of the play to identify the way roles and status can shift through the drama.

Summary

- Code language is the specific vocabulary, syntax or style used by a particular group of people.
- It can be used to bind people to you or exclude them.
- It can be used as **Ethos**, to identify yourself and establish your authenticity.
- It can be used as **Pathos**, to empathise with a group.
- If you look for codes in your character's language, you will find who they align themselves with.

Other texts where you could explore the use of code language with these exercises:

Kwame Kwei-Armah, *Statement of Regret*. In this play, the divisions and affiliations of the group of men are often defined by their vocabulary and dialect, both of which can be forms of code language. Most of the characters partake in code-switching: changing between dialects to strengthen their position within the group or challenge another's.

Robert Icke and Duncan Macmillan's adaptation of George Orwell's *1984*.

Peter Hall's adaptation of George Orwell's *Animal Farm*. With these exercises you can make sure the new political vocabulary is powerfully heard.

Aphra Behn, *The Rover*. The themes of this play are the intertwined worlds of honour, love, money and matchmaking. The language used is steeped in the codes that bind and separate the characters and their desires.

7.

Showing Several Rhetorical Devices Being Used Within the Scene

SPEAKERS USE RHETORIC TO
TRY TO ENSURE THAT THEIR
ARGUMENT IS HEARD.

It's impossible to write a book about rhetoric in plays without looking at Shakespeare's *Julius Caesar*, and in particular, Brutus' and Antony's speeches at Caesar's funeral in Act 3, Scene 2. Risking that I may turn you off completely, I'm going to point out a few more rhetorical devices for you to consider. I wouldn't expect you to remember the names of all these devices but as Shakespeare uses so many of them, a bit more knowledge can only empower you to connect with the characters in this classical Roman world, where rhetoric was so important.

If you are playing either of these roles, I think you would find it interesting to look at the rhetoric in both parts. You may remember that earlier on I spoke of how important it is to listen actively when you are trying to gain ground within a debate or argument. If you are playing Antony you need to have heard Brutus' speech very clearly because you are responding to it. I think you will find it helpful to recognise that both characters would have studied rhetoric as part of their education and they would understand the potential power it carries. They are men who are used to persuading people with their words.

Brutus begins:

> BRUTUS. Be patient till the last. Romans,
> countrymen, and lovers! Hear me for my cause, and
> be silent, that you may hear. Believe me for mine
> honour, and have respect to mine honour, that you
> may believe. Censure me in your wisdom, and awake
> your senses, that you may the better judge. If there
> be any in this assembly, any dear friend of Caesar's,
> to him I say, that Brutus' love to Caesar was no less

than his. If then that friend demand why Brutus rose against Caesar, this is my answer: not that I loved Caesar less, but that I loved Rome more. Had you rather Caesar were living, and die all slaves, than that Caesar were dead, to live all free men? As Caesar loved me, I weep for him; as he was fortunate, I rejoice at it; as he was valiant, I honour him: but as he was ambitious, I slew him. There is tears for his love; joy for his fortune; honour for his valour; and death for his ambition. Who is here so base that would be a bondman? If any, speak; for him have I offended. Who is here so rude that would not be a Roman? If any, speak; for him have I offended. Who is here so vile that will not love his country? If any, speak; for him have I offended. I pause for a reply.

ALL. None, Brutus, none.

BRUTUS. Then none have I offended. I have done no more to Caesar than you shall do to Brutus. The question of his death is enrolled in the Capitol; his glory not extenuated, wherein he was worthy, nor his offences enforced, for which he suffered death.

The first thing to notice about Brutus' speech is that it is in prose. Secondly, it is almost an exercise in rhetoric.

The feeling of prose speech is always more informal than poetry. However, the devices he uses, most of which involve repetition in some form, add a rhythmic element that is more often found in poetry and which can be very compelling. These repetitions could be a striving for balance but they involve quite long, complicated thoughts. Despite the potential for informality within the prose style and although clearly he persuades the crowd (at least in the short term), there is a scholarly and somewhat contrived feeling to the speech.

People who teach this play will be very familiar with its rhetorical cleverness, but in order for you to bring the speech to life, playing a fully owned character, the repetitive elements need to be noticed and strongly used.

I'm now going into more Greek, not to confound you but to highlight the different strategic elements of the speeches. And when I'm talking about rhetorical devices I'm not talking academically or theoretically. I'm talking about careful, considered strategies that concern life and death to the characters you are playing. The stakes are high.

He begins with a device called **epanalepsis**, which is the use of the same word to begin and end a sentence, or thought:

> **Hear** me for my cause, and be silent, that you may
> **hear. Believe** me for mine honour, and have respect
> to mine honour, that you may **believe. Censure** me
> in your wisdom, and awake your senses that you may
> the better **judge**.

'Censure' and 'judge' do not, of course, mean the same thing but there is an implication of judgement in the word 'censure'. Additionally we cannot ignore the aural repetition, the pun within 'censure' and 'sense' which follows the pattern of the repetition of 'honour' in the preceding sentence.

Exercise 33

This exercise will draw your attention to the repeated words and also help you to find the energy you need.

Speak or read this section of the speech and tap the table as you speak the first and last words of each sentence. Be sure to tap on the word, not just after or before it.

Repeat the exercise without the tapping but in the light of it.

I feel that it is essential for the **epanalepsis** to be persuasive. You must be sure that the last word of each sentence lands, for it is there that the power of the repetition lies.

In this sentence Brutus famously uses **antithesis**:

> If then that friend demand why Brutus rose against Caesar, this is my answer: not that I loved Caesar **less**, but that I loved Rome **more**.

The next is **antimetabole**, a reversal of the order of words used:

> Had you rather Caesar were **living, and die all slaves**, than that Caesar were **dead, to live all free men**?

Exercises 22 and 23 are useful to feel the balance of both **antithesis** and **antimetabole**.

This is followed by **parallelism**, when the phrases are structurally and linguistically alike:

> As Caesar loved me, I weep for him; as he was fortunate, I rejoice at it; as he was valiant, I honour him: but as he was ambitious, I slew him.

Then there is **isocolon**, where each clause has the same number of words

> There is tears for his love; joy for his fortune; honour for his valour; and death for his ambition.

Rhythm is a distinctive element of both **parallelism** and **isocolon**, which creates a sense of a journey through the text; a forward momentum that feels compelling and that certainly draws the ear. Here is an exercise to help you to absorb this fully and take your listeners with you.

Exercise 34

Set up a line of chairs, enough for one chair per section. So in the example of **parallelism** above, use seven chairs placed in a line, side by side. Opposite that line, place one chair. As you speak the text do the following:

As Caesar loved me – sit on one of the six chairs
I weep for him – move to the next chair
as he was fortunate – move to the next chair
I rejoice at it – move to the next chair
as he was valiant – move to the next chair
I honour him – move to the next chair
but as he was ambitious – move to the next chair
I slew him – move over to the one chair on its own

With the **isocolon** section, use three chairs in one line and one opposite on its own.

The exercise will help you to be clear with the details of the argument; to feel the forward momentum and also to feel the power of the conclusion.

Repeat the text without the chairs but in the light of the exercise.

Exercise 35

Use the same set-up of chairs and the same journey. This time, if the words spoken are positive, stand up on the chair (or if you aren't very agile, stand in front of the chair). If the words are negative, sit on the chair.

You will probably see that in the centre section you are standing on the chairs a lot, which might give an uplifting, positive feel. This will be sharply contrasted by the downward energy of the last move.

Repeat the exercise without the chairs but in the light of the exercise.

You could also try the exercise moving from chair to chair in this way:

As Caesar loved me, I weep for him – sit on one of the chairs
as he was fortunate, I rejoice at it – move to the next chair
as he was valiant, I honour him – move to the next chair
but, as he was ambitious, I slew him – move to the next chair

Repeat the exercise without the chairs but in the light of the exercise.

I suggest you do the six-chair exercise first, then this one. The first will help you find the detail of the thought, the second will give you strong, structured thoughts.

Brutus concludes this main, persuasive section of his speech with **anaphora**, where there is a repetition of two phrases at the beginning and end of each clause:

Who is here so base that would be a bondman? **If any, speak; for him have I offended. Who is here** so rude that would not be a Roman? **If any, speak; for him have I offended. Who is here** so vile that will not love his country? **If any, speak; for him have I offended.**

Exercise 36

As with the **epanalepsis** at the beginning of the speech, I would tap the table on the first and last words of each sentence.

These exercises also draw our attention to how important it is that you carry your vocal energy through to the very end of a sentence or a thought, not just in this speech but in all your theatre speech. In modern English we tend to lose vocal energy at the ends of thoughts and frequently allow the last word or two to drop off or fade away. If you do this, you will not serve your character's argument or use the power of the rhetorical structure. In short, your thought or argument will not be clearly heard!

With so much rhetoric, why is it that the crowd don't stay with Brutus once Antony has spoken? How does he turn the Plebeian crowd against Brutus.

Let's have a look at Act 3, Scene 2:

> ANTONY. Friends, Romans, countrymen, lend me your
> ears;
> I come to bury Caesar, not to praise him.
> The evil that men do lives after them;
> The good is oft interrèd with their bones;
> So let it be with Caesar. The noble Brutus
> Hath told you Caesar was ambitious:
> If it were so, it was a grievous fault,
> And grievously hath Caesar answered it.
> Here, under leave of Brutus and the rest –
> For Brutus is an honourable man;
> So are they all, all honourable men –
> Come I to speak in Caesar's funeral.
> He was my friend, faithful and just to me:

But Brutus says he was ambitious;
And Brutus is an honourable man.
He hath brought many captives home to Rome,
Whose ransoms did the general coffers fill:
Did this in Caesar seem ambitious?
When that the poor have cried, Caesar hath wept:
Ambition should be made of sterner stuff.
Yet Brutus says he was ambitious;
And Brutus is an honourable man.
You all did see that on the Lupercal
I thrice presented him a kingly crown,
Which he did thrice refuse: was this ambition?
Yet Brutus says he was ambitious;
And, sure, he is an honourable man.
I speak not to disprove what Brutus spoke,
But here I am to speak what I do know.
You all did love him once, not without cause:
What cause withholds you then, to mourn for him?
O judgement! thou art fled to brutish beasts,
And men have lost their reason. Bear with me;
My heart is in the coffin there with Caesar,
And I must pause till it come back to me.

To begin with, Antony adopts Brutus' phrase but shifts it. He begins with 'Friends', immediately placing himself at the level of the Plebeans, as one of them. And his list of three – 'Friends, Romans, countrymen' – has an easy rhythm to draw his listeners' ears. He invites them to *lend* their ears; he does not command them to listen. He is using **Ethos** by presenting himself as their friend and then later as Caesar's friend.

Like Brutus he employs **repetition** and **parallelism** but his most powerful device is the use of a 'refrain'. A refrain is a repeated phrase, or few lines, most often heard in poetry and songs at the end of a verse or stanza. It can reinforce a message contained in the verse or comment on it in some way. Here, Antony subtly shifts the implication of the phrase from praise of Brutus to suspicion of his character.

Yet Brutus says he was ambitious;
And Brutus is an honourable man

And of course Antony, in further contrast to Brutus, is speaking verse. Although his style appears freer and more informal, it is controlled by the structure of the verse line which adds drive and authority to his argument. When working with an actor on this speech I encourage them to enjoy the movement of thought through the line of verse rather than break it up for naturalism. At the same time, I ask them also to feel the balance of the argument contained within the line; the first half against the second. For example:

Friends, Romans, countrymen,   lend me your ears;
I come to bury Caesar,   not to praise him.
The evil that men do   lives after them;
The good is oft interrèd   with their bones;

I ask them to feel that balance without breaking the thought in the line and to trust that this will powerfully enter the listener's ear.

Overall, Antony understands the use and power of **Pathos** when addressing the common man. It is the central strategy of his argument. He describes Caesar in terms of his relationship to himself as his friend ('He was my friend, faithful and just to me') and to Rome (and therefore to his listeners):

He hath brought many captives home to Rome,
Whose ransoms did the general coffers fill…
When that the poor have cried, Caesar hath wept:

He describes how Caesar refused the offered crown three times, and finally he appeals directly to the emotions of the present moment; to that of the crowd and of his own:

You all did love him once, not without cause:
What cause withholds you then, to mourn for him?
O judgement! thou art fled to brutish beasts,
And men have lost their reason. Bear with me;
My heart is in the coffin there with Caesar,
And I must pause till it come back to me.

Yet within this emotional appeal the repeated question about Caesar's *ambition* and Brutus' *honour* is actually an appeal to **Logos**. He presents this as fact and this fact gains strength as he lists Caesar's achievements and motives.

1 CITIZEN. Methinks there is much reason in his
sayings.

2 CITIZEN. If thou consider rightly of the matter,
Caesar has had great wrong.

3 CITIZEN.   Has he, masters?
I fear there will a worse come in his place.

4 CITIZEN. Marked ye his words? He would not take
the crown;
Therefore 'tis certain he was not ambitious.

This Citizen interprets this as **Logos**; as evidence.

1 CITIZEN. If it be found so, some will dear abide it.

2 CITIZEN. Poor soul! his eyes are red as fire with
weeping.

3 CITIZEN. There's not a nobler man in Rome than
Antony.

4 CITIZEN. Now mark him, he begins again to speak.

ANTONY. But yesterday the word of Caesar might
  Have stood against the world; now lies he there.
  And none so poor to do him reverence.
  O masters, if I were disposed to stir
  Your hearts and minds to mutiny and rage,
  I should do Brutus wrong, and Cassius wrong,
  Who, you all know, are honourable men:
  I will not do them wrong; I rather choose
  To wrong the dead, to wrong myself and you,
  Than I will wrong such honourable men.
  But here's a parchment with the seal of Caesar;
  I found it in his closet, 'tis his will:
  Let but the commons hear this testament –
  Which, pardon me, I do not mean to read –
  And they would go and kiss dead Caesar's wounds
  And dip their napkins in his sacred blood,
  Yea, beg a hair of him for memory,
  And, dying, mention it within their wills,
  Bequeathing it as a rich legacy
  Unto their issue.

The will is a master-stroke, and the skill with which he uses
it to excite the crowd puts him in complete control.

  4 CITIZEN. We'll hear the will: read it, Mark Antony.

  ALL. The will, the will! We will hear Caesar's will.

  ANTONY. Have patience, gentle friends, I must not
                                         read it;
  It is not meet you know how Caesar loved you.
  You are not wood, you are not stones, but men;
  And, being men, bearing the will of Caesar,
  It will inflame you, it will make you mad:
  'Tis good you know not that you are his heirs;
  For, if you should, O what would come of it!

4 CITIZEN. Read the will; we'll hear it, Antony;
You shall read us the will, Caesar's will.

ANTONY. Will you be patient? Will you stay awhile?
I have o'ershot myself to tell you of it:
I fear I wrong the honourable men
Whose daggers have stabbed Caesar; I do fear it.

4 CITIZEN. They were traitors: honourable men!

ALL. The will! The testament!

SECOND CITIZEN. They were villains, murderers: the
will! read the will.

Yet before the reading of the will he wants to rouse the
feelings of the crowd even more.

ANTONY. You will compel me, then, to read the will?
Then make a ring about the corpse of Caesar,
And let me show you him that made the will.
Shall I descend? and will you give me leave?

Continuing with his **Ethos** theme that he is one of the
people, he comes down into the crowd and draws them to
Caesar's body.

SEVERAL CITIZENS. Come down.

2 CITIZEN. Descend.

3 CITIZEN. You shall have leave.

ANTONY *comes down.*

4 CITIZEN. A ring; stand round.

1 CITIZEN. Stand from the hearse, stand from the
body.

2 CITIZEN. Room for Antony, most noble Antony.

ANTONY. Nay, press not so upon me; stand far off.

SEVERAL CITIZENS. Stand back; room; bear back.

There, among the crowd and in front of the corpse, he uses the clothes that Caesar is wearing as evidence of the actions of the murderers. Unlike Brutus, who stands above the crowd to speak to them, Antony knows that the evidence of their eyes, when cleverly directed, will move them more than words alone and seal his argument.

ANTONY. If you have tears, prepare to shed them now.
　You all do know this mantle: I remember
　The first time ever Caesar put it on;
　'Twas on a summer's evening, in his tent,
　That day he overcame the Nervii:
　Look, in this place ran Cassius' dagger through:
　See what a rent the envious Casca made:
　Through this the well-belovèd Brutus stabbed;
　And as he plucked his cursèd steel away,
　Mark how the blood of Caesar follow'd it,
　As rushing out of doors, to be resolved
　If Brutus so unkindly knocked, or no;
　For Brutus, as you know, was Caesar's angel:
　Judge, O you gods, how dearly Caesar loved him!
　This was the most unkindest cut of all;
　For when the noble Caesar saw him stab,
　Ingratitude, more strong than traitors' arms,
　Quite vanquished him: then burst his mighty heart;
　And, in his mantle muffling up his face,
　Even at the base of Pompey's statue,
　Which all the while ran blood, great Caesar fell.
　O, what a fall was there, my countrymen!
　Then I, and you, and all of us fell down,
　Whilst bloody treason flourished over us.

O, now you weep; and, I perceive, you feel
The dint of pity: these are gracious drops.
Kind souls, what, weep you when you but behold
Our Caesar's vesture wounded? Look you here,
Here is himself, marred, as you see, with traitors.

Gosh! Does he milk it!

1 CITIZEN. O piteous spectacle!

2 CITIZEN. O noble Caesar!

3 CITIZEN. O woeful day!

4 CITIZEN. O traitors, villains!

1 CITIZEN. O most bloody sight!

2 CITIZEN. We will be revenged.

ALL. Revenge! About! Seek! Burn! Fire! Kill! Slay! Let
  not a traitor live!

ANTONY. Stay, countrymen.

1 CITIZEN. Peace there! Hear the noble Antony.

2 CITIZEN. We'll hear him, we'll follow him, we'll die
  with him.

ANTONY. Good friends, sweet friends, let me not stir
                                          you up
To such a sudden flood of mutiny.
They that have done this deed are honourable:
What private griefs they have, alas, I know not,
That made them do it: they are wise and honourable,
And will, no doubt, with reasons answer you.
I come not, friends, to steal away your hearts.
I am no orator, as Brutus is;
But, as you know me all, a plain blunt man,

That love my friend; and that they know full well
That gave me public leave to speak of him:
For I have neither wit, nor words, nor worth,
Action, nor utterance, nor the power of speech,
To stir men's blood: I only speak right on;
I tell you that which you yourselves do know;
Show you sweet Caesar's wounds, poor poor dumb
                                        mouths,
And bid them speak for me: but were I Brutus,
And Brutus Antony, there were an Antony
Would ruffle up your spirits and put a tongue
In every wound of Caesar that should move
The stones of Rome to rise and mutiny.

ALL. We'll mutiny.

1 CITIZEN. We'll burn the house of Brutus.

3 CITIZEN. Away, then! Come, seek the conspirators.

ANTONY. Yet hear me, countrymen; yet hear me
                                        speak.

ALL. Peace, ho! Hear Antony. Most noble Antony!

ANTONY. Why, friends, you go to do you know not
                                        what:
Wherein hath Caesar thus deserved your loves?
Alas, you know not: I must tell you then:
You have forgot the will I told you of.

ALL. Most true. The will! Let's stay and hear the will.

ANTONY. Here is the will, and under Caesar's seal.
To every Roman citizen he gives,
To every several man, seventy-five drachmas.

2 CITIZEN. Most noble Caesar! We'll revenge his
death.

3 CITIZEN. O royal Caesar!

ANTONY. Hear me with patience.

ALL. Peace, ho!

ANTONY. Moreover, he hath left you all his walks,
   His private arbours and new-planted orchards,
   On this side Tiber; he hath left them you,
   And to your heirs for ever, common pleasures,
   To walk abroad, and recreate yourselves.
   Here was a Caesar! When comes such another?

1 CITIZEN. Never, never. Come, away, away!
   We'll burn his body in the holy place,
   And with the brands fire the traitors' houses.
   Take up the body.

2 CITIZEN. Go fetch fire.

3 CITIZEN. Pluck down benches.

4 CITIZEN. Pluck down forms, windows, anything.

   Exeunt CITIZENS *with the body.*

ANTONY. Now let it work. Mischief, thou art afoot,
   Take thou what course thou wilt!

For an actor, Antony's speech may be easier that Brutus'. There's more of it, of course, and its direct appeal to **Pathos** is a joy to grasp. But I suggest that if the actor plays the repetition of the chorus-like lines –

   Yet Brutus says he was ambitious;
   And Brutus is an honourable man

– as **Logos**, we will hear the clever development of his argument more clearly.

To help this, try these exercises.

Exercise 37

As the actor playing Antony speaks the text, ask the crowd, or any other actor or actors working with you, to repeat these choric lines after he has said them. Ask them to say the lines in an affirmative manner. You may find the crowd's interpretation of those lines will develop as the speech goes on.

Repeat without the crowd repeating.

Exercise 38

This time, instead of the crowd repeating the lines, after Antony has said them once, ask them to join in with him when he says them again.

Repeat without the crowd joining in.

As an actor, I suggest you try to explore the use of **Pathos** and **Logos** as you speak the lines with Exercises 1, 2 and 3.

To help to feel the balance of the thoughts within the lines you could use Exercises 22 and 23, changing your script from hand to hand or moving between chairs with the two halves of the line. Be careful, when you repeat the text without the exercise, that you don't break the thought in the middle but allow the balance to be heard through the flow of the line.

Romeo and Juliet is also a wonderful play that contains plenty of rhetorical devices. Let's have a look at Act 3, Scene 5, and we'll begin with **Ethos**, **Pathos** and **Logos**.

I suggest that the first three speeches in the scene are the characters using **Logos** as their persuading tactic: giving evidence for why they should stay or go.

Capulet's orchard.

Enter ROMEO *and* JULIET *above, at the window.*

JULIET. Wilt thou be gone? it is not yet near day:
  It was the nightingale, and not the lark,
  That pierced the fearful hollow of thine ear;
  Nightly she sings on yon pomegranate-tree:
  Believe me, love, it was the nightingale.

ROMEO. It was the lark, the herald of the morn,
  No nightingale: look, love, what envious streaks
  Do lace the severing clouds in yonder east:
  Night's candles are burnt out, and jocund day
  Stands tiptoe on the misty mountain tops.
  I must be gone and live, or stay and die.

JULIET. Yon light is not day-light, I know it, I:
  It is some meteor that the sun exhales,
  To be to thee this night a torch-bearer,
  And light thee on thy way to Mantua:
  Therefore stay yet; thou need'st not to be gone.

Romeo switches now – is he changing to **Ethos** ('This is who I am and how much I love you') or **Pathos** ('I want you to feel sure of my love')? You decide – or try playing both. Which one works best?

ROMEO. Let me be ta'en, let me be put to death;
  I am content, so thou wilt have it so.
  I'll say yon grey is not the morning's eye,
  'Tis but the pale reflex of Cynthia's brow;
  Nor that is not the lark, whose notes do beat
  The vaulty heaven so high above our heads:
  I have more care to stay than will to go:
  Come, death, and welcome! Juliet wills it so.
  How is't, my soul? let's talk; it is not day.

In response, Juliet returns to **Logos** for her first three lines, in order to persuade him to go. Her topic changes as she rails against the rhythm of nature but she still uses **Logos**.

> JULIET. It is, it is: hie hence, be gone, away!
>   It is the lark that sings so out of tune,
>   Straining harsh discords and unpleasing sharps.
>   Some say the lark makes sweet division;
>   This doth not so, for she divideth us:
>   Some say the lark and loathèd toad change eyes,
>   O, now I would they had changed voices too!
>   Since arm from arm that voice doth us affray,
>   Hunting thee hence with hunt's-up to the day,
>   O, now be gone; more light and light it grows.

> ROMEO. More light and light; more dark and dark our
>   woes! […]

> JULIET. Then, window, let day in, and let life out.

Romeo's responses are now all **Pathos** as he tries to reassure her of their future together.

> ROMEO. Farewell, farewell! one kiss, and I'll descend.

The following speech of Juliet is a wonderful example of **hyperbole**. This is a rhetorical device where the speaker exaggerates to intensify their feeling or their meaning. Juliet, in the heat of her young passion, her first experience of love, finds her life totally absorbed by Romeo. For her, their separation will feel like an eternity.

> JULIET. Art thou gone so? Love, lord, ay, husband,
>   friend!
>   I must hear from thee every day in the hour,
>   For in a minute there are many days:
>   O, by this count I shall be much in years
>   Ere I again behold my Romeo!

ROMEO. Farewell!
I will omit no opportunity
That may convey my greetings, love, to thee.

JULIET. O think'st thou we shall ever meet again?

ROMEO. I doubt it not; and all these woes shall serve
For sweet discourses in our time to come.

Juliet's following premonition is chilling, of course, as we know the end of the play.

JULIET. O God, I have an ill-divining soul!
Methinks I see thee, now thou art so low,
As one dead in the bottom of a tomb.
Either my eyesight fails, or thou lookest pale.

ROMEO. Trust me, love, in my eye so do you:
Dry sorrow drinks our blood. Adieu, adieu!

Now let's see how they hear each other and how their dialogue works. Notice how they choose to respond to each other's argument; which parts of the argument they choose to tackle. To begin with, Romeo responds to Juliet's last word 'nightingale' with his argument of the 'lark', but Juliet's response to him is to his first argument about 'the light':

ROMEO.   Look, love, what envious streaks
Do lace the severing clouds in yonder east:
Night's candles are burnt out, and jocund day
Stands tiptoe on the misty mountain tops.

JULIET. Yon light is not day-light, I know it, I:
It is some meteor that the sun exhales,
To be to thee this night a torch-bearer,
And light thee on thy way to Mantua.

She is perhaps trying to overweigh his final, warning words about the real danger of him staying.

ROMEO. I must be gone and live, or stay and die.

JULIET. [...] Therefore stay yet; thou need'st not to be
                                                    gone.

Use the listening Exercises 16 and 17 to help you hear how their arguments switch and she tries to persuade him to go.

In her final speech, Juliet makes use of **alliteration**.

JULIET. O **F**ortune, **F**ortune! all men call thee **f**ickle:
If thou art **f**ickle, what dost thou with him
That is renowned **f**or **f**aith? Be **f**ickle, **F**ortune;
For then, I hope, thou wilt not keep him long,
But send him back.

See how her use of words beginning with *f* enhances her arguments. At first she is trying to persuade 'fickle Fortune' not to have anything to do with Romeo as he is known for the opposite; for being *faithful*. Then she feels that this very *fickleness* will mean that if *Fortune* takes him up, she will soon let him go again. It continues the push–pull of their dialogue in the scene; the struggle they have to part but knowing they must.

Use Exercises 26 and 27 to help you focus on this use of alliteration.

Then, finally, I should point out Shakespeare's use of **antimetabole** in this scene (see page 136). The balance and rhythm of words and images in these lines enters the ear of the audience and each character. The images reflect their conflict; the dilemma they find themselves in:

I must be gone and live, or stay and die.

More light and light; more dark and dark our woes!

And (echiong the line above):

Then, window, let day in, and let life out.

With these lines, use exercises such as 22 and 23, passing objects between your hands on operative words, or sitting on different chairs. They will help you to physically feel the shifts and balances of the thought.

8.

The Use of Punctuation in Rhetoric

PUNCTUATION CREATES
RHYTHMS TO LEAD THE EAR.

Punctuation is a slippery thing! Like all language and syntax it changes from age to age and varies from writer to writer. But it is always a way of structuring thought and can therefore be a very powerful tool in the persuasion game. If you recognise how it works, it can support the strength of an argument or debate as it can direct both the journey and the focus of thought through the division of sentences. It also creates rhythms to lead the ear. When understood and acknowledged by a speaker, it can help them to reveal the text and not rush from point to point.

Colons and semi-colons are particularly powerful tools with which to indicate how thoughts are structured and debates played out. They are not used so much now; the hyphen and the comma are more popular but less specific. Here's a guide to how they work, and my examples are from Act 2, Scene 6 of *Saint Joan* by George Bernard Shaw.

Colon (:)

Introduces something: a word, a phrase, a sentence, a quotation or a list. (As in the sentence I have just written.)

Yes: they told me you were fools.

It can be used to introduce a sentence that explains, elaborates, restates, proves or undermines what came before:

Light your fire: do you think I dread it as much as the life of a rat in a hole?

It can be used to introduce a sentence that is the fulfilment of a promise made or implied in the previous sentence:

It is not the bread and water I fear: I can live on bread: when have I asked for more?

It can be used between two sentences that are in antithesis:

You promised me my life: but you lied.

Semi-colon (;)

A connector between two related sentences. It separates sentences more strongly than a comma, adding strength to the ideas in the second part of the sentence.

But without these things I cannot live; and by your wanting to take them away from me, or from any human creature, I know that your counsel is of the devil, and that mine is of God.

It can separate the units of a list which is made up of phrases or complete clauses rather than single words.

I could do without my warhorse; I could drag about in a skirt; I could let the banners and the trumpets and the knights and soldiers pass me and leave me behind as they leave the other women.

It can replace conjunctions: *and*, *but*, *for*, *nor*, *or*, etc.

George Bernard Shaw tends to use semi-colons plus the conjunction, but they can easily replace it and still make sense.

The Difference Between Them When Speaking

With a **colon**, the sentences on either side are of equal weight: the second sentence balancing the ideas contained in the first.

With a **semi-colon**, the energy of ideas is moving forward more strongly; the second sentence being a development of the first.

Colons and **semi-colons** keep a thought open: a **full stop** ends it.

A Word of Warning About Commas

It is a textual convention to place a comma before a character is addressed. That could be by name, title or any other form of address; John, Mary, my friend, dear sir, my lord, etc. I would not expect this comma to be considered part of the thought process of a speaker and so not acknowledged in speech.

The writers of English comedies in the Restoration period of history use strong punctuation to great effect. So did Richard Brinsley Sheridan, who revived the genre of the comedy of manners at the end of the eighteenth century. Let's look at a section from Act 3, Scene 2 of his play *The School for Scandal*.

Charles Surface is a likeable younger brother who is known for his extravagant profligacy. Moses is a money lender. They are talking to Sir Oliver Surface who, unknown to Charles, is his uncle. He is in disguise as another money lender, Mr Premium.

> MOSES. Sir, this is Mr. Premium, a gentleman of the strictest honour and secrecy; and always performs what he undertakes. Mr. Premium, this is –
>
> CHARLES. Psha! have done. Sir, my friend Moses is a very honest fellow, but a little slow at expression: he'll be an hour giving us our titles. Mr. Premium, the

plain state of the matter is this: I am an extravagant young fellow who wants to borrow money; you I take to be a prudent old fellow, who have got money to lend. I am blockhead enough to give fifty per cent sooner than not have it; and you, I presume, are rogue enough to take a hundred if you can get it. Now, sir, you see we are acquainted at once, and may proceed to business without further ceremony.

Exercise 39

Reading from these or any other text that uses colons and semi-colons, the exercise is to walk as you read. When you come to a full stop, turn and change direction. When you come to a colon, turn and go back the way you came. When you come to a semi-colon, hesitate, then walk on in the same direction. For this exercise, you ignore the commas.

The exercise works in two ways: it reveals clearly how the thought before a colon sets up what comes after and it is very helpful in finding new energy for new thoughts.

Exercise 40

You can use your script for this exercise.

As you speak the first part of the sentence, before a colon or semi-colon, hold the script in one hand. Change hands when you begin the part of the sentence that comes after the colon or semi-colon. Change hands again when you come to a full stop. This will help you to feel the balance of the thought and how the second part or parts of a thought are developed from or in some way extend the first part.

Read the text again without the hand-changing but remembering the way the thoughts played out.

These exercises are particularly helpful when dealing with older texts, including Shakespeare, where punctuation is often more elaborate and specific than in modern texts.

Summary

- Punctuation is how we structure thoughts in a written text and it is very useful in the rhetoric game.
- When you understand what punctuation marks mean, they can help you to understand the detail and power of a character's argument.
- Using the punctuation can help you to lead the ear of your listener.

Conclusion

WE NEED TO USE LANGUAGE
ACTIVELY TO GET INTO OUR
LISTENER'S EAR.

Whether you are an actor, a director or a teacher, I hope you have enjoyed my way of thinking and working with rhetoric in plays. I hope it will give you the confidence to try out the work I've presented in this book and explore the way characters use rhetoric as they speak their way through the play. I hope the exercises will help you to unlock, not just persuasive strategies, but also something about the characters and the themes of the play.

Aristotle didn't invent rhetoric. What he did do was identify, name and codify the many possible linguistic strategies with which to debate and argue. Some of these, when recognised, are extremely useful for actors. In this book I have spent time on Aristotle's three main strategies, **Ethos**, **Pathos** and **Logos**, because I focus on them a great deal in my work. I have then gone on to show you how traditionally poetic elements of texts can also be used persuasively.

Many of the rhetorical elements of playwriting that I have discussed are taken from the aural, storytelling tradition. The structural elements of a well-told tale can be seen in plays old and new. I like to think of structure as the geography or road map of a journey we are being taken on. Storytelling and balladeering are the predecessors of plays, and those of us involved with the production of modern plays can learn from them. In the same way that we listen to stories, when we hear a play, we are witnesses to the drama of other people's lives, and with luck, we learn from their experiences. Plays are nothing if not storytelling.

In my view, listening is a key element in persuasion. First of all, we need to be able to listen to each other in order to converse, discuss and debate successfully. We also need to make sure we are heard by others, that they listen to us. We need to use language actively to get into our listener's ear. My work encourages the actor to explore the text to find out if their character uses language persuasively. Or perhaps to discover who doesn't listen or persuade well. Then you can begin to ask the question 'Why?' which will lead you to a deeper exploration and understanding of characters and meaning.

I am, of course, a theatre voice coach. My aim with all my work is for actors to speak with clarity, authenticity and ease, whatever their role in a play. I have found the focus on rhetoric to be most effective. Actors have loved discovering the strategies inherent in rhetoric, and the active nature of this work has chimed well with their modern acting technique.

My one note for actors on press night is very often: 'Listen to each other and talk to each other.' That is the essence of rhetoric, the Art of Persuasion.

PLAYS ARE NOTHING
IF NOT STORYTELLING.

Acknowledgements

The author and publisher gratefully acknowledge permission to quote from the following:

A Doll's House by Henrik Ibsen, translation © 1965 Michael Meyer, *The Empress* © 2013, 2022 Tanika Gupta, and *A Raisin in the Sun* © 1959 Lorraine Hansberry, all published by Methuen Drama, an imprint of Bloomsbury Publishing Plc, by kind permission of Bloomsbury Publishing Plc; *Small Island* by Helen Edmundson, adapted from the novel by Andrea Levy, published by Nick Hern Books Ltd; *Death of a Salesman* © 1949 Arthur Miller, *An Inspector Calls* © 1947 J. B. Priestley, and *A Streetcar Named Desire* by Tennessee Williams © 1947 The University of the South, © renewed 1975 The University of the South, all published by Penguin Books Ltd.

Every effort has been made to contact copyright holders. The publisher will be glad to make good in any future editions any errors or omissions brought to their attention.

About the Author

Jeannette Nelson trained as a singer and dancer at the Arts Educational School, then worked in theatre and cabaret for ten years in Britain and around the world. In her late twenties, she took a degree in English at Queen Mary, University of London, and then trained as a voice teacher at the Royal Central School of Speech and Drama.

Jeannette taught for many years at the Guildhall School of Music and Drama, as well as working as a voice and dialect coach in theatre, film and television. Besides the National Theatre, where she has worked since 1992, becoming Head of Voice in 2007, she has been resident voice coach at Shakespeare's Globe, the Royal Shakespeare Company and Sydney Theatre Company, Australia. She has also worked on many productions for other British theatre companies in London's West End and leading regional theatres.

As a voice and dialect coach in film and television, her work includes the films *The Merchant of Venice* (with Al Pacino, Jeremy Irons and Joseph Fiennes), *Kingdom of Heaven* (with Orlando Bloom), *Wuthering Heights* (with Juliette Binoche), *The Hollow Crown* (with Benedict Cumberbatch, Philip Glenister, Keeley Hawes, Sally Hawkins, Tom Sturridge and Sophie Okonedo), and *Romeo and Juliet* (with Jessie Buckley, Josh O'Connor, Tamsin Greig, Deborah Findlay and Adrian Lester).